MEL NURSE

Mr Swansea

*For my wife Marian, and children
Nicola, Andrew and Mandy.*

*And all supporters of my beloved
Swansea City Football Club.*

MEL NURSE

Mr Swansea

WITH PETE WELSH

y Lolfa

First impression: 2009

© Copyright Mel Nurse, Pete Welsh and Y Lolfa Cyf., 2009

The contents of this book are subject to copyright, and may
not be reproduced by any means, mechanical or electronic,
without the prior, written consent of the publishers.

The publishers wish to acknowledge the support of
Cyngor Llyfrau Cymru / Welsh Books Council

Cover design: Robat Gruffudd

ISBN: 9781847711472

Published, printed and bound in Wales
by Y Lolfa Cyf., Talybont, Ceredigion SY24 5HE
website www.ylolfa.com
e-mail ylolfa@ylolfa.com
tel 01970 832 304
fax 832 782

Contents

This book is primarily about football. From the moment I entered school it was all I thought about. Hence, this book is not about my private life or business life. That is a different story altogether, although my life in football has helped me progress enormously in my property business. I can't mention everybody's name, but they will know who they are and I have truly valued the support they have given me over the years.

Mel Nurse

1

The Swansea School of Excellence

I ALWAYS SAY I WAS born lucky – in terms of the time and place I was born into. Financially I wasn't, but with regards to what was to become my life – *football* – I was.

I was born in 1937 in an area of Swansea called Fforestfach. My father came from a village out in the country called Penclawdd and my mother came from Cwmbwrla, which is in Swansea. How they met I don't know. In those days there were no vehicles on the road, it was horse and cart, and bicycles. If you had a bus you were lucky – one every five hours or whatever – so how they met I couldn't tell you. Anyway, they got married and I was born in a one-room property in a place called Newbury House. It's still there now and about four years ago it came on the market and I nearly bought it. I was looking at it, thinking, "Jesus, I was *born* there!" But of course you mustn't allow your heart to rule your head so eventually I decided against it.

The war started in 1939 when I was two years old. We'd moved to Cwmbwrla to a two-up two-down and my mother struggled through the war years to pay the five-shillings-a-week rent. My father was in the army and was away for many years. When he came home he had £80 gratuity money which he spent gambling on the horses. At that time we could have bought the freehold on the house for that figure.

My mother would pick me and my brother Tony up from school, take us home and we'd have a bath in front of the big open fire. There was no central heating, no electric, just a gas lamp. She'd have two big kettles boiling on the hob so there was always hot water for a cup of tea. At four o'clock every day she'd go out the back and fetch a big galvanised bath that was hanging on the wall which we'd both sit in – that's how small we were.

We'd go to bed straight after our bath. We had overcoats for bedclothes as we couldn't afford blankets. I can remember waking up many mornings with my leg down the sleeve of the coat! There were black blinds covering the windows that came right down during the blackout. I got up one morning quite early, must have been six o'clock, and opened the blinds. I looked across the road where there were two houses totally blown out. I was so young and naïve to what was going on around us that my first thought was, "Cor, we've got somewhere to play". Fancy thinking that! What about the poor people who were in the house? They must have been killed. It only happened the once, but we had the floodlights going around all the time. We were only 300 yards or so from the Cwmfelin Steelworks up by the Maltsters which the Germans were trying to hit, so there were houses disappearing all over the area. It was a lovely community though and everyone really stuck together.

We had moved when I was a couple of months old from Fforestfach to Alice Street in Gendros, or Cwmdu as it's sometimes called. I went to school in Cwmbwrla, and *what* a school it was – I have to emphasise this. Today football clubs have a 'School of Excellence'. They're a fantastic idea and they have to have them in order to compete, but in our days the schools did it themselves. The teachers put themselves out tremendously and they looked after you. It was *so* different. I'm not saying they wouldn't now but the system has changed so much that teachers can't put themselves out for a child like they did in my day. The schools can't afford to take sport to that level anymore in case anyone gets injured. At the time of writing we've had the worst winter in nearly twenty years and we've got parents complaining that the schools are closing because of the weather. But those same parents would be the first to sue the school if their child broke an arm or a leg. *You can't have it all ways.* The safety of children is the priority, so I think the schools are doing right.

The boys from Alice Street

There was no money around, during and just after the war – *no money*. People talk about a recession now but hey, we were living in a recession then and you didn't know there was one on!

A lot of famous footballers came from Alice Street itself, though of course they weren't famous back then. They were all about my age – John and Mel Charles, Len O'Shea, Ernie Jones (he was a little bit older), Jackie Roberts. There were seven or eight who would all go on to be full internationals. It's unbelievable how one street, which numbered about thirty houses, could produce that many senior international footballers. We all went to the same Cwmbwrla School. It was 200 yards from home one way, with the Charles brothers 200 yards the other. Unbelievable. What an environment to be brought up in! So that's what I mean when I say I consider myself very lucky to have been born at that time.

Cwmbwrla Park was in the centre of everything. It was the base for all us kids who would congregate there. Looking back at it now it was fantastic but we didn't really appreciate it. Only after the time goes by you realise how fortunate you were.

We didn't have a football of our own as they were too expensive, so we'd play with a tennis ball in school. When I went from the infants to the junior school that's when football started taking over, and on a Saturday we'd have a real football to play with. The teacher would bring it over and it was like *gold!* It was small, made of real-leather with a lace on top and an inner-tube. When it got wet it was like a medicine ball. They couldn't play with it now but of course we didn't know any different. You can kick a ball for miles today; you have to kick it with restraint and not as hard as you can. If a keeper kicks a modern ball from the edge of the box as hard as he can it'll go straight into the other keeper's hands. In our days they'd give it everything and it would only reach the halfway line!

I've always been a forceful person – in football anyway. Not in real life. I was certainly never top of the class but I wasn't dull either. I just wasn't interested in being clever, or reading or things like that. I failed the 11-plus – I just wasn't a very knowledgeable person. A lot of kids were like me and weren't interested in learning, but once they realised their potential they progressed and many became geniuses in their own field. I just enjoyed taking part in sport: long-jump, javelin, throwing a cork ball as far as you could; and I captained the cricket and the football teams. I took to the latter especially. When I was 14 I was invited to go up for trials for Swansea Schoolboys; prior to that I had no knowledge of football other than playing it locally and for Cwmbwrla against teams like St Joseph's.

I was a big boy and able to look after myself. At senior school in Manselton I started playing with the seniors in my first year. A teacher from each school in the area would select one or two boys to represent Swansea at schoolboy level. Mr Morris from our school chose me and sent me to go for a trial. I came out of school at dinner time, jumped on a bus in Brynhyfryd and got up to Ynystawe Park, a lovely big open area. There'd be about forty boys there from all over Swansea, and the main man at the time was Mr Dai Beynon. He was big, six foot four tall and very stern, but he knew what he was doing. Looking back I can put a value on it. He understood that at schoolboy level you need big, strong lads and you pick the best from that category. Of course you get some genius small lads but Mr Beynon believed in the need for the bigger variety. I was lucky I fitted the bill.

We played once a week, on a Tuesday, and Mr Beynon would chop and change the players, sending you on for half an hour or whatever, so you didn't have long to shine. At the end he'd get up on a box and say, "Right, I want half of you to come back next week." That was about twenty boys, and he'd always call my name in the middle of the recalled boys so the wait was agonising. The first six or seven names would be called out and I'd be praying and praying.

Ashleigh Road to Wembley

I was selected though I wasn't a permanent fixture in the team. But then I was 14 playing with boys of 15 and there was a lot of quality about. (I can't mention all the names in case I leave someone out, which would be wrong.) Home games had been played down at Ashleigh Road, but they started playing at the Vetch Field in my first year. This was the first time I went down the Vetch Field, linked to the schoolboys. I didn't know anything about the Swans and had no idea there was a football ground down in town! Swansea then had all different little communities and I didn't know that area. Neither did my friends, as we never went out of our community – that's the way it was.

My parents knew nothing about football and they didn't push me into it because there was no money in it! Personally I wasn't interested in watching football; it was all about playing for me. I thought, when the years have gone by and the legs stiffen up – that's when I'll watch it!

I was involved in a few Swansea Schoolboys games in my first year and became a regular in my second year at 15. That's when I also started playing for the Welsh Schoolboys. We played against England in front of a packed Wembley Stadium. We drew 3-3 against a side that boasted Bobby Charlton and Wilf McGuiness, despite being down to ten men, or boys, for much of the game.

We would compete at schoolboy level for the English Cup. If you were to see it you could hardly believe it: a big silver cup with the names of past winners around the base. Well, Swansea Schoolboys seemed to have won it every other year, it was *incredible*. The quality of players coming from Swansea just after the war was unbelievable.

At this time the careers officers would come to school and help guide you into whatever direction you wanted to go. I wanted to be a carpenter – I love carpentry – and I was always top of the class at woodwork. Like sport, I achieved at it because I had a love for it. If I'd loved other subjects I might have achieved at those too. I don't *think* so, but who knows! I sometimes think my life was planned because the two things I had a flair for – football and carpentry – are the only two things I've ever needed to have a good life.

So at 15 I was having to decide what I wanted to do for a living. It had to be football. The problem was that while four clubs wanted to take me on – Arsenal, Bristol Rovers, West Bromwich Albion and one I don't recall – having seen me perform for both Swansea and Wales Schoolboys, I didn't want to leave Swansea. But Swansea Town didn't want me. There were scouts everywhere; John Charles had been taken off to Leeds and other lads were taken off all over the country to different clubs, but I didn't want to leave home. I was very fortunate that I had good parents and my brothers and sister as well. We lived close to the bone, struggling like everybody else was, but I was happy and I didn't want to leave my family behind. I wasn't going anywhere. I didn't care who they were. Football was a sport to me; I never envisaged it as a living.

My father's shoes

I didn't have my own suit; I couldn't afford one. Or my own shoes. If it was a dry day I'd wear gym shoes to school and if it was wet I'd wear Wellington boots. They were great for playing football in the yard because you wouldn't slip. That's all the footwear I had. When I got selected to play for Swansea Schoolboys I had to borrow my father's shoes, along with his suit and his watch, and whenever I travelled around the country my mother would give me the rent money. She'd say, "Son, just for you to have money in your pocket, take this with you ... *but try and bring it home.*"

Only twice did I not bring it home. The first occasion was with Swansea Schoolboys, playing up in Ilford in Essex in the semi-finals of the English Cup. We'd gone up a couple of days beforehand and Mr Beynon, who was in charge, got us all together and took us to the Serpentine in Hyde Park. We had boys from all over Swansea, one of whom was Muzzo Cook who came from Mumbles. Now Mumbles was a fishing area, with rowing boats and what-have-you, so Muzzo said, "I know all about this water lark, I'm from the Mumbles." Of course I'd never been in a boat before, but the one Muzzo went out in had a hole in it and promptly sank. So much for Muzzo and his nautical expertise. We all had to chip in for the damage and new clothes, so that was the first time I failed to bring all the rent money back.

The second time, I'd found myself over in Ireland with the Welsh Schoolboys side. We still had food rationing back at home and I always remember how scarce food was: two-ounce of this, two-ounce of that. I was only too aware of what was available to you. But in Ireland I found tins of this, tins of that – *everything* was plentiful.

So I spent the rent on tins of corned beef and salmon! By the time I got home I was beginning to worry what my mother was going to make of this suitcase full of tinned food instead of the rent money. We'd just moved from Cwmbwrla up to a newly-modernised council house in Penlan. I walked in the door and my mother was standing there. Luckily she was in a good frame of mind. Before I'd even had chance to say anything, she said, "Son, I've got some good news for you," which I was grateful for as I was becoming increasingly concerned as to what she'd make of my purchase. Then she said, "There's a scout here from Swansea Town."

Glyn Evans

The scout's name was Glyn Evans, though he was nicknamed Glyn 'Buff'. He was a lovely fellow, a bit on the plump side. Well, I couldn't believe it. Just imagine how I felt. I hadn't wanted to leave home although four clubs had wanted me, but I'd been told Swansea Town didn't want me. I've been excited a few times in my life about things that have happened to me, but I can't put into words the way I felt about this. It was 1952 and Swansea Town were in the old Second Division. They were a force, with players like Rory Keane, Tom Kiley, Roy Paul, Billy Lucas, Ivor and Len Allchurch, Cliff Jones, Mel Charles, Terry Medwin, Des Palmer and many more.

They'd sent Mr Evans up to see me but I was in Ireland, so he stayed at my parents' house for two days because he lived up in the Rhondda. Within a matter of months after he had brought me to the Vetch, that same gentleman, a lovely jovial fellow, was leaving town on a bus back up to the Valleys. On the dual carriageway at Fabian Way a low-loader was coming in the opposite direction. Its crane suddenly got loose, took the top off the bus and decapitated him. Very sad.

It seemed like all the clubs in the country were after the Swansea Schoolboys; we had such a great side. We'd won the English Cup and come runners-up in the Welsh Shield one year, then vice versa the following year. Everyone wanted these great players – Willsy went to Chelsea, Ronnie White to Leeds – they were going everywhere. Nobody was going down the Vetch, but I couldn't join the Swans quick enough. The moment I signed for Swansea Town a lot of the other lads followed suit.

I didn't want to leave home at 15. It's not right and I would not encourage kids to do so because I don't think they are mentally prepared at that age to be taken out of their familiar environment. It's asking enough of them to try and achieve, without putting them in a hostel or wherever. Only one or two that went away in my day were successful. Everybody has a choice of two roads to go down and I suppose I've been very lucky in selecting the right road.

2

Down the Vetch

I WAS 15 YEARS OLD and it was my first day with Swansea Town. There were eight youngsters – a few from the previous year and four of us new boys. Straight away we were doing the groundwork, sieving on the pitch and really mucking in. Afterwards we were sitting in the tin shed at the back of the Centre Stand with the groundsman sitting opposite with his assistant. He suddenly asked me to go to the main office and bring him this or that – to this day I can't remember what I was told as my mind went blank with the fear of having to go into the office.

That was the type of person I was then. My knees started knocking at the prospect of it! I thought, I'm not going in there, the manager's in there, *no way*. Well, the groundsman could see I was terrified and if I hadn't shown my feelings he may have sent somebody else in, but he insisted I face my fear. So off I went, down the tunnel and under the old Centre Stand, up the couple of steps and into the offices. I opened the door quietly and a gentleman sitting behind a desk looked at me. It was Mr Hoskins, the club secretary at the time, and to his left the treasurer, Mr Harvey. "How can I help you, son?" he asked. I was so terrified in this situation that I forgot what I'd gone in there for and could only stare back vacantly.

Billy McCandless' office

Fortunately for me the team manager at the time was Billy McCandless. The doorway to his office was just beyond Mr Hoskins' and was open. He was only a small gentleman, stocky, baldy (just like me now!) and he was sat there in his swivel chair drinking whisky. He always drank whisky; pissed as a parrot he was. It was a different time altogether! "What do you want, son?" he asked. Oh God, the bloody manager was speaking to me now so I was really trembling. Then he turned to Mr Hoskins and said, "Trev, what are we paying him? What's he on a week?" "One pound, two and six, boss," came the reply. *"Well give him two weeks' wages."* I hadn't gone in for money; I still couldn't remember what I'd gone in for! Mr Hoskins gave me two pounds, ten shillings, and I ran home. I didn't go back to the groundsman and the rest of the boys. I ran straight back to Penlan, five miles uphill.

When it snows in Swansea, Penlan really gets it. Cwmbwrla is down at the bottom of the mountain and would have nothing, but Penlan is at the top and it would be six feet deep. We had moved to Penlan in 1946 and the year after was the coldest winter on record, but because of my age it was wonderful. Anyway, back to 1952, my mother looked out of the window one day and said, "You're not going working down the Vetch today, the snow is too deep." She went across the road to use the phone and inform them that I couldn't get in through the snow. (Only one person in the street had a phone in those days.) She spoke to Billy McCandless, who was living on Carmarthen Road in Fforestfach. He said, "You tell him to get in here now. *I've* got in so you tell him to get down here!" Of course there was no snow in Fforestfach, and once I'd waded through and got to

Cwmbwrla, sure enough there was no snow. So he was quite justified to haul me in.

Billy McCandless was around for twelve months before he died. It was a similar situation to Glyn Evans. Mr McCandless loved pigeons, as a lot of people did in those days. People who were interested in sport could quite easily be interested in pigeons too, as they were something you could enjoy around the house or in the garden. People didn't drive here and there for recreation as they couldn't afford it. He used to go home to his house in Fforestfach where he had his pigeons in a shed in the back garden. One day he climbed up on the roof of the shed, possibly on whisky, and fell off to his death. He must have been in his sixties.

Billy McCandless was a good manager, a quality manager. He took Swansea, Newport and Cardiff up to the old Second Division. And he selected me, so he must have been good! I found out later that when I was playing for Swansea Schoolboys, the popular belief among the staff was that I wouldn't make the grade. Billy McCandless thought differently; he had seen me playing and he wanted me down there. The whole thing started through him sending Glyn Evans up to Penlan.

Where's the ball?

I quickly realised that all you did as a youngster with Swansea Town was work on the ground. It was nothing to do with football! Your daily routine would be sweeping the stands, clearing the North Bank and the toilets. We'd have to be down the Vetch for eight o'clock. In the summer months we'd be wheeling barrows of soil into the ground so they could re-turf the pitch. Of the eight of us on the ground staff, there would be six working outside and two inside – one in each dressing room, cleaning boots and taking the kit to the cleaners in Richardson Street. They would assess you and then put the two youngsters they considered most likely to progress on the inside. I was outside for a year and then graduated to the inside. It was good experience and the senior players wouldn't look down on us as they had done their stint themselves and knew what it was like. It just rolled on like a cycle once you were part of the club, and it was a lovely feeling. We used to watch the full professionals training while we were sweeping the terraces. The only training you did was on Tuesday and Thursday evenings; running around the Vetch and playing football on the beach. You could, if you wished, go behind the North Bank at dinnertime and kick a ball around on the concrete, so we'd do a bit of that before we went back to work. But you weren't kicking a ball around the pitch, that's for sure.

If you were in that situation at 17 you were lucky, because there were many lads who were good enough to become full-time professionals but weren't taken on because the club simply couldn't afford them. They already had forty professionals on the books in those days. Football clubs weren't organised in a commercial fashion like they are today, where they use every avenue available to generate income. In the 1950s a club would survive solely on gate money, and even though you only played once a fortnight you'd still have two weeks' wages. We'd have 28-30,000 gates in those days but it was only thruppence or sixpence a time to get in. So although there were forty pros on the books, they were paying them peanuts.

All I lived for was football. I'd be down the local park all day and in the evening when I wasn't down the Vetch, then I couldn't go to bed early enough. I'd be in bed by nine just so the next day would come around quicker and I'd be down the Vetch for training. I *loved* training.

For home games the Vetch would be full to capacity and every ticket would be spoken for. But as ground staff lads we could sit on a bench on the track at pitchside – that is if we made it back from playing in the morning in time to watch the first team. You wouldn't be able to sit in the stands because there was money to be generated with those places. Everybody associated with the club was given a blazer which we would have to wear with a collar and tie for home games. With all the millions the players earn today they somehow still manage to dress like hobos. I liked the formal dress because it showed respect, but I dressed like that so much through my football career that I seldom wear a suit these days. Watching the Swans in the early 1950s in front of a full house and knowing you were going to be a part of it was a dream. The home side and the visitors had brilliant players on the field – *brilliant*.

Swansea Town in those days had four teams: the first team, the Combination, the Welsh League, and the Colts. I'd gone from the Colts up to the Welsh League, playing against the likes of Ton Pentre, Gwynfi and Caerau – good, quality teams, and by God they would give you a game – and I was knocking on the door of the Combination side. The Welsh League would really bring the youngsters on. The money in the game obviously wasn't like it is today, and the income to the clubs certainly wasn't either, but in terms of the culture of the day it was massive. Not many people had television and everybody supported football.

Ice Cream all round!

We had moved from the council house in Penlan to Gendros, and Les Bailey lived two doors away. He worked for the local paper, the *Evening Post*, which gave great coverage to the Swans. It was a Friday evening when Les came around and told me that my full first team debut was to be against Leicester City at the Vetch the following day: 24 March 1956. On hearing this, my mother went out and stopped the ice cream van to buy everyone in the street an ice cream!

I got in the side because the regular centre-half Tom Kiley was getting over a broken ankle, plus he was getting on a bit. If he'd been young and fit they wouldn't have looked at me for a few years. The new manager Ronnie Burgess was playing himself in those days. He'd been brought to the club by Billy McCandless, and after Billy's untimely demise they made Ronnie player-manager.

I got down there on the day of the game and sat in the dressing room with all the senior players. They began filing out to see Bernard Sherrington, the physiotherapist, and on the way down to his room there was a shelf on the side with glasses of sherry lined up on it. It certainly wasn't like today where they watch what you eat and want to know everything – they bloody time you when you go to the toilet! In our days it was just a sport: you would train in the week, go home and do whatever you want; you could get paralytic if you wanted to. As long as you performed on the Saturday they didn't give a monkey's. I was a bit wary of the senior players as I'd been cleaning their boots for a couple of years, so I thought I'd better take a glass of sherry as well just to fit in. I'd never drunk anything before so I didn't feel that comfortable afterwards. We won 6-1 nevertheless!

We had two away games after that and I was very shy travelling with the first team at 17. I was happiest following the group and wouldn't push myself forward. We went to Doncaster Rovers and I played against a lad called Alick Jeffrey, a whizz-kid who captained the England Youth team and was dubbed the 'English Pele'. I had played for the Welsh Youth against England Youth down at Milford Haven when Alick and I were the captains. Unfortunately he broke his leg young and it changed the course of his career forever.

During the game against Doncaster, a ball was pumped into the corner and Alick and I both ran for it. Alick got there first and went to whip a cross in, and I instinctively closed my eyes and shielded my face. When I opened my eyes I realised he'd put the ball through my legs and gone around me. I was left staring at the crowd of spectators. I could have died looking at the supporters' reaction to me. If I'd had a shovel I'd have dug a big hole and buried myself. After that I never flinched from a ball ever again; you could hit it at me point-blank and I would keep my eyes open. A few years later at Wembley against England, Bobby Charlton volleyed the ball from outside the box; he caught it beautifully and my Wales team-mate Terry Hennessey dived out of the way. It hit me straight on the chest. I didn't want to show the 100,000 crowd that it had hurt me, so I put on a brave face and walked away. The ref blew for half-time a few minutes later and when I got my shirt off in the dressing room, I had a panel on my body with the imprint of the ball on it.

When we played Doncaster they had a centre-half

called Charlie Williams, one of the first black players in the game. He got stuck in during that match. He's best remembered for his career after football, as a popular turn on *The Comedians* in the 1970s. After the game we went back to the hotel and sitting there in person was Freddie Trueman, the cricket maestro. He was waiting for the lads, because in those days all the sports people got to know each other. I couldn't speak to him because I'd heard of him on the wireless; he was a legend all over the country and there he was sitting with us in the hotel!

In every game I was learning something. I didn't do badly; I basically did whatever I had to do. I was a big lad even at 17 and I wasn't afraid to face anybody. I believe that when you go on the field you all go on as equals, then after about ten minutes you can assess your opponents and adjust your game accordingly. Even if I was facing John Charles I'd have gone about it the same way.

At the time Cardiff City had a player called Stan Montgomery who was getting on a bit but was available for a small fee, maybe £5,000. Swansea Town were rumoured to be interested in his services but they decided to put me in instead of signing him. For whatever reason, I don't think the regular centre-half Tom Kiley ever came back.

3

The Call-Up

IWAS 17 AND A half and had got into the Swans first team, but then at 18 I was called up for National Service. If you weren't a tradesman you got called up at 18, but if you had a trade they allowed you to finish learning it and then join at 21. I was fortunate to go in at 18 as I hadn't met any women, so I was a free agent with no commitments of that kind.

The boys who had learnt a trade and went in at 21 were courting and in some cases were married, so it was a different proposition to going in at 18 like I did. Imagine being 21 or 22 with a wife and maybe even a child back home and being sent away – *that* was real hardship. I wasn't a tradesman, although I had started with Griff Davies in Paxton Street as a carpenter. But because I wanted to be a footballer, I left after two months.

When I left Swansea to join the Royal Engineers I was already familiar with travelling thanks to various footballing trips, but for the first time in my life I was going away without knowing when I'd be coming back home. When I arrived in Worcester I was among 200 other boys of a similar age, all stood there not knowing one another or what was around the next corner. We were shaking with the uncertainty of what was happening to us.

We were all designated into different units, 40 lads in each, and told to get onto some huge lorries. This was the time when the Teddy Boy fashion was all the rage – big suede shoes, drainpipe trousers and large drape coats topped off with the Tony Curtis haircut. (I had plenty of hair in those days so that's what I looked like!) We jumped up on the wagons which had six-foot-high wheels, but when you're 18 you're so alive and active that you're literally bouncing. From the station we were driven up to the camp which consisted of a series of billets, or 'spiders' – long corridors with shed-like buildings at the end of each, hence their nickname. When I got in I made a bee-line for the bed furthest from the door, but another bloke who must have been more nervous than me beat me to it. Bernard Davies his name was – and he was from Swansea! We'd seen each other on the train to Worcester but had thought nothing of it.

Professional footballer?

Once you'd put your baggage down you had to report to a hut, again forming a long queue outside with no idea what's awaiting you. It came to my turn so in I went, to be met by a sergeant, corporal and lance-corporal sitting behind a trestle table. The sergeant asked my name and I said, "Mel Nurse, sir." Then he said, "What did you do in civvy street, Nurse?" I told him: "Professional footballer, sir." He said, "There are no professional footballers in this lot – move along!" So I moved along sharpish as I was shaking with tension anyway.

I went to the next hut to get my 1157 form, a document you need to get issued with all your kit. Out of there and into another bloody queue, again wondering, what next? A voice was screeching out loud: "LEFT, RIGHT, LEFT, RIGHT, LEFT!" Two regimental police were marching this poor sod who had no laces in his shoes and no belt on, so his trousers were falling down as he was trying to march along. Well, being a bit nosy, I strayed a little bit from the queue to see what all the commotion was about. The sergeant saw me and screamed, "COME HERE YOU!" and sent me off all over the camp picking up litter. When I eventually got back in line I noticed all these recruits going in one door looking like Tony Curtis and coming out another door, bald and crying. This was all within two hours of getting there. It was terrifying.

The following day, the commander of the regiment posted a lot of notices on the notice board. We were told that anything on that board overruled anything else you'd been instructed – never mind what the corporal or sergeant had told you. Once you'd read your name on the board, that's what you abided by. So I saw my name up on the board: 'NURSE – REPORT TO THE PLAYING FIELDS 2PM.' I went to see the corporal to consult him about it. He told me: "Forget about it." I'll never forget his name – Smith. You don't forget these situations because you're scared stiff all the time. He sent me to the square where they were trying to teach us all how to march. Our new boots were absolutely killing us and there were bodies going to the left, bodies going to the right; we were all over the place! All of a sudden a voice from off the square ordered us to stop. A sergeant appeared and marched around the square, before asking, "Which one of you is Nurse?" I put my hand up. "Me, sir." He marched up to me and put his face right in mine. I was shaking in my boots by this stage. He said, "Why aren't you in the playing fields? Don't you read regimental notices?" All I could say was that I'd planned to go but the corporal had told me not to. Well, the sergeant about-turned from me and went straight for Corporal Smith and laced him in front of everyone on the square. He was bright red *and* puce at the same time somehow; he nearly died!

It wasn't over yet, though, because the sergeant turned back to me and barked, "Get your kit on and get down to the playing fields NOW!" I was so excited that I forgot all about what the corporal must have thought of me, and I sprinted off the square. Again he stopped me in my tracks: "Nurse, you MARCH off the square!" So I did, but once I was off I bolted to my billet and put my gym shoes, shorts and stockings on – probably in that order – and ran through the camp. I'd been there three days and hadn't even seen a football, so when I ran onto the field and a ball was rolled to me, I hit it so hard it was probably the best goal I'd ever score in my life. I hit it from the halfway line right into the top corner.

Little did I know at the time but the guy who'd rolled the ball to me was Dave Mackay, who of course would go on to be a legendary player with Tottenham Hotspur. He was at Hearts at the time (up in Scotland), just a kid like myself, though maybe two or three years my senior. As soon as the sergeant saw me hit that ball, he said, "Right, you can go back on the square now." He'd just wanted to see if I could play and I'd obviously shown him.

Another guy I would play against in regimental games was George Kirby, who would go on to play for Swansea Town. George was a couple of years older than me and was kicking me all over the place. Dave Mackay was alongside me in defence and said, "If you don't kick him back – *I'll* ****ing kick you!" So I started kicking George as it was a better option than getting one off Dave!

Then I got the news that my unit was being posted to Hong Kong, which was regarded as the best place you could be posted to. But because I played football they wanted to keep me in the country, so they sent me on a ten-week advanced course in Aldershot to become a corporal. After you'd passed out there they'd send you to other camps to train other people. That's how it worked. I was sent down to Fleet in Hampshire where our camp overlooked the aerodrome with the Red Arrows flying over. It was a fantastic place, and a bonus of being there was that I was guaranteed to get home to Swansea every week if I wanted, courtesy of a kindly superior called Major Stone.

AWOL

Occasionally Swansea Town would get me off so I could come back and play for the first team. One instance was when the Swans were playing Fulham at Craven Cottage at the start of the 1956/57 campaign. I had to get up from Hampshire to Paddington to meet the team; they'd be arriving from Swansea by train and there would be a coach waiting for us. I didn't have a pass to get out of camp so I went out the back gates in the early hours of the morning without anyone knowing and ran the four miles to the station in my uniform. I caught a train up to Paddington and as soon as I arrived at ten o'clock, I fell asleep. Now if any military police had seen me sleeping on the station in my uniform they'd have hauled me in on suspicion of going AWOL – which I had done so they'd have been right!

When I woke up and looked up at the big clock, I saw it was dead-on one o'clock, which was the time I was meant to be meeting the rest of the team. So I got up and ran around looking for them. To my horror, I suddenly realised I was at *Victoria*, not Paddington. *I was at the wrong bloody station!* I ran down to the tube and looked on the map for Putney Bridge. When I got there, I could see the floodlights of the Fulham ground in the distance. I made a bee-line for the lights, no messing around, but by the time I got there the rest of the players were on the field. They'd already given in the team-sheet to the referee so I was left sitting there watching the game in my uniform. But once it began I thought, thank God I was late, because Fulham had Johnny Haynes and Jimmy Hill and they beat us by seven goals to three. What a team they had! The Swans had just signed Derek King from Spurs who was a centre-half like me. The first ball he had to deal with he headed back to the keeper who missed it. That set the tone for the rest of the afternoon. In fairness to the club, they didn't blame me for being late; they allowed for that if you were in the forces.

One of the last times I got out of camp to play for the Swans was at Bristol City in April 1958 when we needed a win to stay in the Second Division. They had their legendary player John Atyeo turning out. We'd just signed a player by the name of Pat Terry who was outstanding in the air. He didn't have to run, he'd just leap from nothing. Again I was supposed to be playing, so I left camp and headed up to Reading where I'd get a connection to Bristol. So far so good, then I got on the Bristol train and it stopped at every bloody station. It was the paper train. I was watching the time go by until in the end I was up behind the engine pushing it!

I got to Ashton Gate late again and sat on the bench alongside our manager at the time, Ronnie Burgess. Lennie Allchurch put the ball over and Pat Terry headed it home. We won 2-1 and everyone on the bench was crying with happiness as we stayed up by that one goal. The excitement was unbelievable. You've got to live through these things to appreciate them.

I was on a retainer from the Swans while I was in the forces: five pounds a week. My mother was having that and banking it for me. I was also getting one pound, two and six from the Army, which was brilliant for me. In my opinion they shouldn't have done away with National Service; they should have it now – it would right society. It was the experience of a lifetime; you are in situations you never forget and you learn from them. I hated every minute of it but I'm glad I did it, if you can understand that. Although I wouldn't have been a Teddy Boy or a troublemaker if I hadn't done it, it definitely changed my attitude to life.

4

First-Team Regular

A FTER BEING DEMOBBED IN April 1958 I came back to Swansea, back down the Vetch, and picked up where I'd left off two years previously. I was on £20 a week with the club. All my family were working – my two brothers, sister and my parents. My father was earning a bit more than me, in the steelworks, and my brother was earning the same as me working on the railways. So as a footballer I was earning pretty much what the average working man earned. That puts it in perspective, doesn't it?

Even internationals like Ivor Allchurch, Cliffy Jones and Terry Medwin were earning £20 a week, so you simply can't compare it with today's standards, not even with what the lower league professional footballers earn now. The thing is, in our day the directors ran football clubs as a sport, not as a business. Today they're run as a business because they have to be. The television has taken it out of all proportion, I feel.

I was 21 years of age and living in a council house in Gendros. One evening my father had been out to a friend's house and was told about a small cottage for sale in that area. When he came home he just casually mentioned it to my mother and myself, saying it was going for £800. I couldn't believe it, but later that night we went to have a look at the cottage and found it was true. But where were we going to get £800 from?

I liked cars and had always bought them through the higher purchase system. At that particular time, and for the first time in my life, the car outside on the road was my own – paid for. I went back to the garage that I had bought the car from and they agreed to put it back on higher purchase so we could raise the money to buy the cottage. It took three months to purchase and on completion we moved in. It had outside water supply, dry toilet, two rooms upstairs and two rooms downstairs. We would be saving £3.50 rent per week!

At this same time I was selected to play for Wales against England in Cardiff, my first full international (see next chapter), and here I was working on the cottage, trying to make it liveable for us to move in. One day I was upstairs knocking down the ceiling of the ground floor. Someone called out: "Mel?" but it was too late – I had pushed the ceiling down not realising there was someone standing in the doorway. It fell to the floor and a big cloud of dust gushed through the whole house, with the person in the doorway catching the full blast. It was Tudor James of the *People* but I couldn't recognise him; he looked like Al Jolson – all you could see were the whites of his eyes!

The half-back line

On my return to the team from National Service, the manager moved me from my favoured centre-half to left-half because they'd signed Ray Daniel from Cardiff City. He was from Plasmarl and a was great player who was coming home with this move to Swansea. He'd experienced everything with Wales and had been a legend at Arsenal and Sunderland, but he was coming to the end of his career and the novelty had worn off for him – let's put it that way. He still had unbelievable ability though. They moved me to left-half because I was fit and I could run all day. If we were playing against Huddersfield, for instance, who had Denis Law, they'd put me on him because he would run everywhere. If we were playing against Fulham they'd put me on Johnny Haynes, so they were using me as a donkey.

Trevor Morris was now manager and I went in to see him to explain that I'd far sooner be playing centre-half. "What are you moaning about?" he asked me. "You're in the first team. You won't get in the first team at centre-half, we've got Ray Daniel playing there now." I protested that I didn't want to play left-half and I didn't care whether I was playing for the first team, second team or the Colts, I just wanted to play centre-half. He promptly shoved me in the reserves! Fortunately for me there were some great players in the reserves, including Brian Hughes at right-half and Malcolm Kennedy at left-half. The three of us struck the right balance: Brian liked going forward with the ball and Malcolm was an intelligent player who liked to sweep in behind and clean up.

At this time the first team were at the bottom of the table and the reserve team were at the top of the Combination. Trevor Morris then took the whole half-back line out of the Combination and put it in the first team. We went nineteen games without defeat! Unfortunately we actually ran out of games; a couple more and we'd have won promotion. (Naturally the Combination team slipped down the table.) The manager was very clever by taking the three of us into the first team as a unit. The whole philosophy wasn't as technical as it is today. It was: if you're in trouble, get behind the ball. In many ways it's too professional now. They've taken the sport out of it and replaced it with science.

Toward the end of my National Service I was working in the camp clothing store where I was never pushed for time and could do pretty much what I wanted. I remember sitting there when it came on the wireless that the Manchester United team plane had crashed. Within a month of that they began borrowing players from clubs to replace the ones they'd lost in that terrible accident. If clubs could afford to they'd help them out by loaning them players. During this rebuilding process it was very fortunate for me that the Wales manager Jimmy Murphy was also assistant to Matt Busby at Old Trafford, so he was well aware of me from coming through the Welsh ranks. In the wake of the disaster, Murphy was left in charge of United while Matt Busby was in hospital. (They recently unveiled a plaque in Murphy's native Rhondda to recognise his achievements and he's still revered at Old Trafford.) Colin Webster and Ken Morgans would come from United to Swansea Town, and during their restructuring they organised a friendly with the Swans at the Vetch.

Which Mel?

It was a full house and a wonderfully entertaining game, ending 6-4 to the visitors. I wasn't aware at the time but one of the reasons they had organised the game was for United to run their eye over me and see how I'd perform. After the game I saw the headline in the paper:

'UNITED MAKE OFFER OF £35,000 FOR MEL.' Well, Mel Charles was playing alongside me in those days and there'd been a lot of talk about selling Charlo around that time. This is what Swansea Town did in those days: they'd sell a player for good money every season to balance the books. Ivor and Lennie Allchurch, Cliffy Jones, Terry Medwin and Des Palmer had all gone, and Mel Charles was rumoured to be next. We'd all gone out after the game to socialise, so you can imagine Charlo – he was the king, Manchester United wanted him! But then he read the small print and saw it was Mel *Nurse* not Mel *Charles*. Well, he didn't speak to me for weeks!

There hadn't been any talk of me going anywhere as I'd only just got in to the first team, whereas Charlo was established, so you could understand the confusion. It didn't sink in at the time. I also didn't realise that Manchester City had been watching me for a while. We'd played Burnley away and lost 2-1; I scored from a free kick. We'd stayed in the Queens Hotel in Manchester, then coming home we were staying in a hotel in Buxton. We travelled everywhere by coach; they were draughty and it would take days to get to your destination. We got to the hotel and paired off to go to our rooms, then a hotel porter called out: "Mr Nurse? *Mr Nurse?*" I looked at him as if to say, how do you know me? He handed me a telegram and as I went to open it a crowd of football reporters from various national newspapers appeared and started to crowd around me. I tried to hide it and ran like hell out of the hotel. I ran through a park and into a telephone booth where I could look at it in private. It said, 'Please phone this number' but I still didn't have a bloody clue what it was about. When I rang I found it was a newspaper asking me if I'd write a column for them when I signed for Manchester United! Well, I didn't know anything about it because back then as a player you weren't kept informed. I knew there had been an offer of £35,000 but the club wouldn't tell you what was going to happen to you, or give you any hint for that matter. I don't know what went on there, to be perfectly honest.

You had no option of going anywhere while you were under contract then, unless the club wanted to get rid of you. The only way you could get out of your contract was by going to the Southern League; you couldn't go to another Football League club.

Roofing the North Bank

When I was a youngster working on the ground staff at the Vetch, the North Bank was a big, open terrace with no shelter at the back, so they decided to cover it. A contractor from down Llanelli way called Zammit had the job and he sub-contracted a lot of the Swans players to work on it as part-time labourers. Can you imagine that today? Cliffy and Bryn Jones, Len Allchurch and myself, among others, worked on putting the roof on during the summer months. We didn't have to report down the ground during the eight or ten-week close season and we were so poorly paid that we took the job on. We'd take the sleepers off the bank and dig out the footings to put the stanchions up. The steelwork and the girders would come in then, though that was nothing to do with us as we weren't steeplejacks. It was brilliant! It kept us fit and healthy and we were earning money. I doubt many people know that the early work roofing the North Bank was done by the actual players of the time.

That terrace was built in such a way that it would cantilever over the back to take more people. It could hold ten thousand, maybe more, at one time. Thirty-odd years later, the part that was cantilevered over the back was corroding. That was why they put the barriers up in the mid-1980s and cut off half the bank, so you were only ever standing on solid foundations. When you'd been familiar with the original depth and what a full North Bank looked like, you noticed the difference when they shortened it. Mind you, by then the crowds had gone away!

Around this time they put floodlights in at the Vetch too. We played our first floodlit match against Hibernian who had a legendary forward at the time called Joe Baker. Why we played Hibs I don't know. It would have been Trevor Morris who decided that, so maybe he had a connection with them.

A good innings

The football season ended earlier in those days. You would be off from April until July, so I played cricket during the summer months solely to keep fit. Some said I was better at cricket than football. I played for a local Swansea league team called Highbury and in one season over the summer we played eighteen games, winning the lot. If Mel Charles was home he'd also play for us, and with other guys like Charlie Caswell we had a very good team. We won the championship and the cup that particular campaign. The club presented me with a cork ball for being the best bowler. I've still got it somewhere.

Each year there would be a charity match at St Helen's

between a team made up of Glamorgan and the All Whites (Swansea Rugby Club) versus the Swansea Town boys. The likes of Jim Pressdee played for Glamorgan *and* the Swans, so there was quite a crossover. If you could play football you were quite likely to be useful on a cricket pitch too. Norman Lawson was a prime example of this, as was Harry Griffiths. You may remember Tony Cottey, who turned out for Swansea City before becoming quite an accomplished cricketer with Glamorgan, though this was many years after my time.

I'd had such a good season with Highbury that I was pretty confident going into this charity match – so confident that I opened the bowling and didn't even bother to take my jumper off. I took a wicket in the first over and thought the next one would be nothing more than a formality. Next at the crease was a small, elderly gentleman. I thought, who's this? But he hit me for six with the first ball. Nobody hits me for six! You can't do that! Off came my jumper and I thought, right, I'll show him. BANG – another six! He hit two sixes and three fours. He was a great player called Gilbert Parkhouse and he hit me all over the park. I was an amateur playing against a professional and had got carried away with myself. A few years later on that same pitch, Garfield Sobers famously hit six sixes, so I was in good company at least!

Through the Brandenburg Gate

We won the Welsh Cup in 1961 and qualified for the European Cup Winners' Cup. We had to go through the Brandenburg Gate into East Germany and play both legs against SC Motor Jena over there, because they wouldn't allow them out of the country to play a leg in Wales. We played one leg in Linz in Austria and one in Jena itself – the two games in the space of two days. We had three big taxis, like limousines, ferrying us through the gate. There were massive girders in the ground to stop any oncoming traffic; you would simply have no chance of getting through. In West Germany it was clean and tidy with waterways and greenery – very nice. But once you were through the Brandenburg Gate it was derelict and filthy with bombed-out buildings everywhere, Russian soldiers walking about with guns, and tanks on every corner.

We stayed in a hotel which had been taken off the owners when the new regime took over after the war. They were now running it for the government. It's hard to imagine now but you couldn't even speak freely – you dared not use your own free expression. On the first day we came out of the hotel and went into a café nearby. Remember we were young guys, a football team, so we were quite excited and behaving as we would normally. Our interpreter, who was a woman, was horrified and told us to keep quiet. Two couples who were in there were looking at us in amazement. It was frightening.

I can't remember much about the two actual games, but I know we drew in Austria and then lost the second leg in East Germany heavily. We went out 7-3 on aggregate. On the final day the three big taxis came to take us back through the gate and there was a rush of twenty people to get in the first one. We couldn't get out of the place quick enough. I think we trampled all over the manager Trevor Morris to get in there! We had lost the two legs but we really weren't concerned. We had a good team: Noel Dwyer, Reg Davies, Colin Webster – all internationals – but the Germans were a strong side and we were frightened to death over there anyway.

Marching orders

I've only been sent off twice in my career. The first time was against Sunderland at the Vetch Field. They had a great team and were going for promotion to the First Division. Big Charlie Hurley, what a player he was! Prior to this I'd played a game for Wales against Northern Ireland at Wrexham which we'd won 2-0. Ian Lawther was centre-forward for both the Irish and Sunderland, so we had two encounters in the space of a few days. After fifteen minutes the Swans were three up against the visiting Rokerites on a particularly heavy pitch. I put a tackle in on the halfway line and gave a foul away, then got up and walked away. As I did so, Lawther got up and ran after me, kicking me up in the air. I got up and, well, I hurt him. If I'm honest, I wasn't thinking and the referee was right alongside me. He said I had to go, so I was off the pitch with the game barely fifteen minutes old.

I came off the field and sat in the dug-out by the manager, but I was so involved watching my lads slide about in the mud in what was a hell of a battle that I forgot the rules of the game. I was shouting, "Come on, Ref, get me back on!" I think I must have pre-empted the sin bin by about forty years! I honestly believed I was going back on until the Sunderland boss Alan Brown leaned over and said, "You might as well go and have a bath, son, you're not going back out there!" How brain-dead can you get? But that's how involved I got in the game. It eventually finished 3-3.

Another time we played Sunderland, we needed a point from the game to stay up and they needed a win to go up. We drew 2-2 and went for a night out down Mumbles Pier to celebrate. It used to be heaving down there in those days and people would queue five abreast to get in. I got down there late-ish and who's in the queue but all the Sunderland players – Charlie Hurley, Brian Clough, the lot of them. "Get us in, would you Mel?" they shouted. I took them in through the restaurant, the back way. It was great then; you were all friends.

Another time we were playing away at Plymouth Argyle and we went down to Devon the night before, which was unusual for Swansea as we normally travelled down on the day of the match. We decided to go to the cinema to see *West Side Story*. I was only 20 or 21 and I liked Westerns – films with a good gunfight. The other players convinced me we were going to watch a cowboy film so I was all for it. I found myself in the picture house and all of a sudden there was all this singing. I was gutted and got up and left immediately. The others knew it was a musical so they had a good laugh.

Roy Saunders' top tips

If you wind the clock back fifty years you'll realise Swansea Town had a number of Irish players. Every pre-season the club would go on a tour of Ireland, playing four or five games to see what talent was over there. On one of the nights off we arranged to go to the dog track and, although I'm not a gambler, I agreed to go along. Most footballers are gamblers in one form or another – or at least back then they were. Roy Saunders loved a flutter. Before each race he'd leave the rest of us standing on the bank and weave his way down through the crowds to where the dogs were waiting in their starting pens. He'd listen to the dog-handlers talking, then come back up to us and everyone would place a bet on the information he had gleaned. I didn't get involved as I thought it was a waste of money.

Roy's information proved useful, as race after race they kept winning. On the sixth and final race I thought, I'm missing out here, this is pretty good. I only had a fiver in my pocket and decided to put it on Roy's tip. He said, "It's either going to be number five or number two." It was the only time he came back and wasn't sure. Still, I was fairly hopeful my fiver was going to come back fifteen or twenty quid. I bet on number two. Number five won. That's my luck with gambling. I'm useless, so I won't gamble at all.

Sadly, Roy Saunders recently passed away. He lived for football just like me. In that sense we were in the same mould; he'd watch his food, go to bed early and all that stuff. He enjoyed a bet but he was totally dedicated to the game, playing at left-half alongside me. When he came from Liverpool to Swansea his first game was at Cardiff. In those days it took ages to get there; we had to go through Neath, Briton Ferry, Port Talbot and all those places. We stopped in Cowbridge at the Boar Hotel where Roy met up with us from Liverpool. That was the first time we met him. After that he stayed in Swansea, occasionally working for the football club, and was very well thought of by everyone in the area. His son Dean played for the Swans (as you all know) and is now manager of Wrexham.

5

Playing for Wales

THE VERY FIRST GAME I played for Wales was against England at Ninian Park. I'd captained the Welsh Youth team and the Under-23s but now, aged 21, I was called up to the first team. It was a hard step up as there were strong, experienced senior players. England had the likes of Billy Wright and Stanley Matthews – it was frightening to think about them.

It was also Brian Clough's first full international appearance for England. Every time I'd played against Cloughie at club level he'd sneaked away from me and scored. He used to get thirty-odd goals a season so he was bloody good. Whether you liked him or not there was no denying he was a good player. What was often termed as his arrogance was in fact pure self-confidence. It wasn't arrogance at all, because he proved himself in whatever he did, whether as a player or a manager.

You can see from the team photo taken just prior to the game that I'd 'Vaselined' my hair flat to my head as I didn't want any getting in my eyes playing against Cloughie! The occasion was overwhelming and I believe the attendance was the largest ever at Ninian Park for a Wales game. Bobby Charlton, Jimmy Greaves – they were all there. (Funnily enough, I was born on exactly the same day as Bobby Charlton – 11 October 1937. His fault he's English!)

I was looking at Cloughie and thinking, "If he goes to the toilet I'm going to follow him and lock the door". That was my frame of mind. England kicked off and Ronnie Clayton and Bobby Charlton passed it back and fore before it went out of play. Now Cloughie was supposed to drag me in at the throw, push me back and then run into space, but I wasn't letting him out of my sight. So as the ball was thrown to him I put six studs straight down his back. He went flying through the air with the shirt almost torn off his back, but it was so quick and unexpected the referee couldn't quite believe it; he just gave a free kick when I should have got a red card. I got away with it because the game was barely two seconds old. I hadn't intended to hurt Cloughie but my nerves and awareness of his ability made it an automatic reaction. He didn't get on the score sheet though and the game ended 1-1. Cardiff's Graham Moore, who was only 18 or so, got the goal for us. We both came in together for our first game, and because we did our jobs at both front and back, we went on to play more games for Wales.

Big John

With all the Wales players at different clubs across the country, the Welsh FA would arrange for us all to meet at a central location when there was an away game and we would travel as a unit from there. When we were going up to Hampden Park to play the Scots in 1959 we met at Lime Street Station, Liverpool. I remember waiting with a cup of tea as some of the others arrived, like Phil Woosnam from West Ham and Vic Crowe from Aston Villa, then we boarded our train to Glasgow. The station up there was a big, domed affair with loads of platforms, so we found it a bit strange that there wasn't a soul to be seen when we got off the train. Under the clock, though, there were hundreds of people surrounding this one person. We thought, what the hell's going on there? It was 'Big John' Charles who'd flown over from Italy and was waiting for us. He was stood there with his Juventus tracksuit on and his holdall. He looked like a bloody giant! He must have felt terrible as there were hundreds of people gawping at him; it was embarrassing. Of course nobody noticed us so we pushed ourselves through the crowd just to be recognised and said, "Hello, John!" He picked up his bag and we headed for the hotel.

At Hampden Park there were so many thousands of fans swarming around the main entrance that we couldn't get the coach in. The police horses, which were so huge they were like elephants, made the crowd part and the bus crept through slowly until we got to the players' entrance. As I was leaving the bus with the police holding the crowds back I saw Bobby Reid, a young lad and colleague of mine at Swansea. The chances of this were a million to one as he'd left the club and gone back to Scotland. We greeted each other and went into the stadium where we had a knockabout on the billiards table. It was good to see him, though it was only brief as I had to go and get ready. Sadly that was the last time I ever saw Bobby. I was having such a good time I forgot we had a game on and I had to be called into the dressing room. I walked in and there was John changing; he had his foot up on the side and was pulling his socks up. He was dark brown from being in the Italian sun and you looked at him and thought, "Bloody hell." Honestly, you can't imagine it – he was so young and active he looked like Mr Universe!

In came Jimmy Murphy with Jock Stein, the Scotland manager. They'd been having a great time drinking whisky. "Jim, see you later!" said Jock. "Cheers Jock!" Jimmy replied. Best of friends. Then the door closed. "Scottish bastard," said Jimmy. Ha ha!

That was the time Mel Hopkins the full-back broke his nose. Scotland had a corner, Johnson took it and we had Jack Kelsey in goal. The ball came across and Mel went to head it away, but Ian St John went up for it as well. WHACK! Mel went down and everyone walked away as they couldn't look at him. Mel was an attractive bloke with thin features and a pointy nose, but this challenge totally crushed it. Doc Hughes came on with Jack Jones, the trainer, and they carried him off on a stretcher with their heads turned away, unable to look at him. I saw him after and all he had was three pieces of skin where his nose had been, as the bone structure had gone. He's had trouble with his nose ever since and has had operation after operation. You don't notice it too much now but it definitely changed his appearance. I've seen a lot of things in my time but that was nasty.

Today you see players going down holding their leg and trying to con the ref, then get up and walk away when he waves play on. They try to get their fellow professionals sent off, but in our day we tried to protect each other. Even if the other fellow had gone over the ball deliberately you still wouldn't try to get him sent off. Mind you, another reason we didn't try that is because if he's off the pitch you can't get your revenge!

I think John Charles scored in that game, a deflected free kick off Dave Mackay in the Scotland wall. It finished one each. John was such an idol over in Italy that no matter what he did or said it would be met with universal applause. He had a deep voice, a real Welsh voice, and he used to sing *Old Black Magic*. I never heard him sing but most probably it would have sounded tidy. He was top of the charts in Italy, anyway.

The best centre-forward in the world?

I was privileged to play against some legendary players for Wales – Derek Dougan for Northern Ireland being one. When we went out to Spain for ten days, looking for revenge for a defeat at Ninian Park, I played against Alfredo Di Stefano. He was a legend with Real Madrid and he was supposed to be the best centre-forward in the world. I played against him twice and didn't think he merited that accolade. During the game in Madrid, the ball came over and I whipped his legs from under him. There were 100,000-plus in the stadium and they threw everything at us. Fortunately all the seats had cushions on them so I was lucky to escape serious injury! We drew 1-1 in Spain and I changed shirts with him at the end. I still have it to this day. I played twelve games for Wales and I was grateful to play each one; to represent my country at all levels was a privilege.

I've done so much travelling with football that I've never been on an actual holiday. Only once did I *attempt* to go on holiday. A friend of mine, Alwyn, and his wife Myra had a caravan on the Isle of Wight and they went every year. They were always going on about how great it was. So one year I said, "Okay, we'll come with you." I didn't want to go but we went all the same. They allocated you a caravan on the size of your family and, although it was only my wife and two children with me, I told them we were a family of eight. I didn't want a box caravan, I wanted a tidy-sized caravan if I was going to go. Anyway, we got over there and I spent the first night standing over my son Andrew (who was about three or four) all night because he gave me the impression he was dying. I created havoc down there, took Andrew to the doctor in the morning then jumped in the van and drove home to Swansea. That's my one experience of a holiday! It just doesn't appeal to me and I'm very lucky that my wife feels the same. I don't know if I've brainwashed her but we're just very happy in Swansea.

Getting back to the Welsh national side, look at us now under John Toshack. I'll be honest: I've had my ups and downs and differences of opinion with him, but nobody could do that job better at this present moment. He had a lot of stick after the defeat to Finland in March 2009 and I thought that was diabolical; the Finns were an old, experienced team and Wales were just young kids. Wales were pushing the ball around and it looked lovely, but it wasn't going anywhere. Finland were in total control of the game. For Craig Bellamy to say after the match that they were "two bad teams" was wrong, because to play for your country you must have quality – you're no mug. I know he was disappointed but you shouldn't make comments like that. This young Wales team will go on for another ten years, so let's remember that.

6

Away from Home

I BOUGHT MY FIRST HOUSE in Swansea a week or so before they transferred me to Middlesbrough in October 1962. Some people believed I asked for a transfer from Swansea, but that obviously wasn't true because you don't go and buy a house and then move. You certainly didn't in *those* days …

My attitude at the time was that if I was lucky enough to own my own house at the end of my playing career, I would have done well. I had no idea what I'd do after football but I certainly never thought I'd end up living in and running a hotel!

I was totally dedicated to football. I've never smoked and I didn't drink until I'd practically finished my career. I wouldn't sleep with my wife after a Tuesday if I was playing Saturday. "No, no – top and bottom sheets, love." I even postponed our wedding for a month because it clashed with a rearranged game against Manchester United. That's how dedicated I was to the game.

Middlesbrough

Fourteen days after I'd bought the house, I was told: "Sign for Middlesbrough or you don't play football again." Firstly, I couldn't understand how the club could turn down £35,000 from Manchester United then accept

£27,000 from 'Boro. Secondly, why would Trevor Morris sell me to a club in the same division?

Players were not knowledgeable about transfer dealings in those days. Even though they are more aware now, they are of an age where they are not experienced business-wise, and who are they dealing with? Business people; *experienced* people who can take advantage of you. So I'm all in favour of players' agents. People say the agents are spoiling the game, but they're looking after the interests of the player. Of course I know they get good rewards, but the player ultimately benefits as well.

I had no idea Swansea Town were about to sell me. I knew about the Manchester United offer and that their rivals City were watching me, but as far as I was concerned it was the kind of paper talk a footballer has to accept. This particular morning I was in Swansea when the club physio Bernard Sherrington came looking for me. He'd been up to my mother's and to my house in Tycoch where I was living at that time. He eventually found me looking for furniture for my new house in a salesroom. "Hello, Bernard," I said, a little surprised. "Oh, Mel," he said, "I've been looking everywhere for you – the manager wants you down the Vetch urgently." I was confused. "What does the manager want with me?" I asked. "You'd better get down there now and find out."

I used to get down to the Vetch at nine o'clock in the morning for training and I'd do ten laps before anyone else came in. It was about 8.30 when Bernard found me, so I was on my way down there anyway. However, because he'd told me it was urgent, well, I'm the kind of person who does the reverse in those situations. I didn't have to be there until ten, so that's when I got there.

We had two trainers at the time: Walter Robbins and Steve Levy. The first person I saw was Walter, who reiterated what Bernard had said. "Where have you been?" demanded Trevor Morris when I walked into his office. "Why? It's only ten o'clock now!" I replied. "Never mind," he said. "Now, get a pair of boots and get up to High Street Station and take a train to Paddington – there will be people to meet you up there." So I said, "What are you on about? I'm not going anywhere. I don't understand, it's Friday – what's this all about?" He said, "I want you to sign for Middlesbrough. They've made an offer for you, we've accepted it, and you're going there." This is exactly how it went down in that office. I said, "I'm not going anywhere, *least of all Middlesbrough!*"

I had travelled up to Middlesbrough before and it seemed like the end of the world. It took an age to get up there on the coach! I wasn't judging the place itself, just its location which was a long, long way from home. "I'm not going to Middlesbrough. I'm not signing for anybody!" I insisted. "Mel, *you're going to Middlesbrough.* Get your boots and go, otherwise you don't play football again." That was the ultimatum he gave me and I honestly believed what he said. As I left the Vetch Field everybody was talking about it; they were all buzzing but I was caught in the middle of it all.

We had a guy working on the ground staff called Monty, a lovely, placid guy who did all the DIY stuff around the place. One of his relations was a director of the Swans called Danny Williams, so Monty advised me to go and see him before I did anything, insisting that the directors of the club didn't know what was going on with regards to my transfer. I had to pass his house to get to mine in Dunraven Road anyway, so I jumped in my car and headed up there. "Come in, Mel," he said. "Son, we don't know what's going on. I haven't heard anything about this so do me a favour: don't sign anything. If you want to sign for them you can do it tomorrow or the day after, but *don't sign anything today* – give us a chance to see what's going on." I promised him I would go and see the Middlesbrough people and acknowledge them, as it was a compliment that they were interested in me, but I wouldn't sign anything that day.

What's happening?

I told my wife what was happening, then set off from Swansea High Street Station on my own. I was familiar with Paddington because whenever we would play a London club we'd go there by train, then on to a hotel by taxi for some food before going to Chelsea or Charlton or wherever. I was met by Bob Dennison and Harry Green, the manager and secretary of Middlesbrough AFC. We shook hands and from that moment I didn't know whether I was coming or going. I told them I appreciated the interest they had shown but that I couldn't sign as I'd promised somebody I wouldn't. I told them I hadn't discussed it with my wife either, so they promptly got her on the phone! They took me to a little side-street café outside Paddington where they pressurised me to sign on the dotted line at one minute to midnight. This brings me back to what I said earlier about players needing agents – they couldn't have treated me like that if I'd had proper representation. I didn't get a signing-on fee, not a penny, but that's how they did business in those days. It was outrageous; I'd just gone from Swansea to

Middlesbrough when I didn't want to, for nothing, and would be on the same £20-a-week wage.

This all happened late into the night and I got to bed at 3am in a London hotel. I was up just two hours later, being taken to Kings Cross station where we boarded a train to Grimsby. I was still holding my boots which I'd had in my hands since leaving the Vetch Field! We arrived at a hotel on the front at Cleethorpes where I was quickly introduced to some of my new team-mates: Alan Peacock, Mick McNeil, Gordon Jones – all internationals. From there we headed to the ground, and went out and played. The ground at Grimsby is on a slope and though we were playing uphill in the first half, we raced into a 3-0 lead. Somehow they pulled level in the second half. Late on, the ball came across into our penalty area. Everybody went up for it but it hit me and went right up in the air. By the time it came down there were twenty-two players waiting for it! We broke away and scored to win the match 4-3. My fault really, for heading it up in the air and setting it up, if you like.

After the match it was back to the hotel, then back to Paddington and Swansea. What a journey! I'd had no intention of going to Middlesbrough, but somehow I'd signed and played for them already. I'm very fortunate that my wife never complained about my livelihood, even though neither of us wanted to leave Swansea. After a couple of days sorting things out, we headed up to our new life in Middlesbrough. The journey up in my Rover 105 took 14 hours, and when we arrived at the Studley Hotel I remember telling my wife: "Right, that's it – we're never going home!"

The Middlesbrough team train at Redcar beach, so that was where I reported the following morning. Like

Swansea Bay, Redcar can often be sunny but it's never as warm up there – it's absolutely freezing. I remember getting the ball and I was tackled so hard straight away that my legs went from under me. So I was sitting on the beach, looking up at this player who'd just 'introduced me' to life at 'Boro and asked him, "What are you doing?" He replied, "*Get up, you Welsh ****.*" I just looked at him and didn't say anything. I didn't even know his name. He kicked me again, so BANG – I hit him on the chin. The coach, Harold Shepperson, who was Alf Ramsey's main man in the England set-up, had told them to have a go at me to see what my response would be.

It was so different up there. As well as Redcar, 'Boro had a second training ground. Swansea had the beach as their second ground, which is where we would do all our ball training. The Vetch was only for doing laps. I could run all day back then and I really enjoyed it. Shepperson split us up into teams to do some relay running, since he liked to vary the training. As I was one of the fastest he put me in with some of the slower players. There was a young lad called John Cliff who was not yet in the first team but was a professional at 18. He'd never shown any sign that he was a fast runner, so they paired him up with me and another young lad. I was a bit cocky at the time and allowed them a head-start, but I overtook them with ease. All of a sudden, young John accelerated and went past me as if I'd been standing still. I'd never seen anyone run so fast! I tried to catch up with him but he had a good thirty metres on me. When I completed the lap I staggered in and he was waiting at the finish line. I walked up to him and hit him hard on the chin. I said, "Son, if you can run like that and you've not let on about it, you've been cheating the club and you've been cheating yourself. You should either be at bloody White City or the Olympics." What a waste. I couldn't believe it. I've run with some fast lads but nobody could touch him.

Nurse – captain

Within two days of settling in, I discovered 'Boro had signed a young lad called Billy Gates. Every club in the country was after him as he had captained England at all the youth levels. I learnt that he was earning £50 a week with £3 living allowance. This was more than double what I was earning, so I didn't like that. He was only a kid, in at right-back behind me. I tried to show him who was boss but he threw it back in my face. Again, BOP! I hit him on the chin. The next day the team-sheet went up: 'NURSE – CAPTAIN'.

The first thing I did when I joined 'Boro was to go and see the club secretary and instruct him to take £10 each week (half my wages) and send it home to Lloyds Bank in Swansea. He asked me how I was going to live but I told him not to worry – I'd survive. As I'd been made club captain, the press in the North East would be looking to me for stories. Len Shackleton, one of the past legends from that area, was writing for a local paper. Every third week I would receive a phone call to let me know he was coming to see me. For the information I supplied him, I would receive a payment of around £30. It was only every three weeks as they would alternate each week between myself, Charlie Hurley of Sunderland and Stan Anderson, the Newcastle skipper.

When I joined Middlesbrough, Brian Clough had just left the club to go to Sunderland. It was a different world then: players would go from one of the big three clubs in the North East to another and it wasn't a big issue. Middlesbrough used the money from the sale of Cloughie to buy me. The stories I heard about him when I got there were unbelievable. He practically dictated to the club, which you can well imagine because he was the king up there. Never mind what he achieved as a manager, as a footballer he averaged thirty goals a season. Like Jimmy Greaves, he was a goal-poacher who just had a knack of being in the right place at the right time. It's a gift. I'd played against Cloughie on numerous occasions, year in year out, and every time I played against him he scored a goal – no more than one, but always one and it was basically my fault. Each time I faced him I marked him very closely, knowing that the previous game he'd scored against me. But he was very clever and he'd sneak away. It was a case of, where's Cloughie? Then all of a sudden he's at the far post and BANG! – he's scored again.

Many years later when I'd finished my playing career, I was up in my apartment above the hotel. A young gentleman booked in and sat himself down at the bar where I've got a number of framed pictures of my playing days. My daughter was serving and the young guy enquired, "Who's this playing football, then?" She replied, "That's my father." "Is it now? *My* father used to play football too," he said. "Who's your father?" my daughter asked. "Brian Clough," he replied. "Brian Clough? My father played against him!" she said. It was Brian's son, Simon.

Unlike his brother Nigel, Simon turned away from football and was doing well for himself. He picked up the phone and phoned home: "Dad, I'm in Swansea …"

Cloughie said, "What are you doing down there, boy?" Simon said, "I'm in this hotel and this young lady says her dad played against you." "Oh yes," said Cloughie, "what's his name?" "Mel Nurse," said his son. "The dirty bastard!" he came back with! You could say that then; there was a bond between players from that era. Well, my daughter and his son burst out laughing. It was only when I came downstairs later on that she told me what had happened.

Mel Nurse – fugitive from the law!

Not long after I'd signed for Middlesbrough in 1963, I drove out to Stockton-on-Tees to the cinema with my wife. There's a ring-road in Stockton with a huge central reservation in the middle. Apart from a Wednesday, when it had an open market, it was used as a car park with hundreds, if not thousands, of cars. After the film we walked back across the car park and as we approached the car the police suddenly came from nowhere, with blue lights flashing all around. At the time the Great Train Robbers had broken out of jail and one of them, Ronnie Biggs, had been spotted on the run in the North East. I looked a bit like him; we both had dark wavy hair and were a similar height. I also had a dark blue Jaguar which was similar to his. The police spread-eagled us over the car, my wife one side and me the other. I was looking across at her not knowing what the hell was going on as they kicked my legs apart. My wife was shaking like a leaf and so was I. Luckily for me, I always used to wear my club blazer and this helped one of the policemen recognise me. I don't know if Ronnie Biggs *was* up there, but it wasn't me, that I do know

– though a lot of people have said that's where I made my money from! Three or so years ago a friend of mine from Swansea, Paul Murphy, went up to Old Trafford to watch a game and in the programme they had a quiz question which was: 'Which footballer was accused of robbing a train?' Answer: 'Mel Nurse.'

Middlesbrough is a lovely place and the people were fantastic. They did everything they could for me and my wife. Ayresome Park was a fantastic ground and really well looked after. As I mentioned, it was significantly colder there. In one game at Sunderland we had to turn our backs to the wind because hailstones like marbles were coming at us. But the worst weather I've played in, ironically, was with the Swans up at Bradford City. Because we had travelled all that way the manager was adamant that we played. It was so cold, nobody could even stand up properly. I have never played in conditions like that, before or since. We went out on the pitch and the referee was uncertain whether to go ahead with it. "Dicey," he said. Our manager didn't go out on it; he just looked at it and said, "What are we waiting for?" Well, the goalkeeper couldn't even run to kick the ball. For me, it was the biggest farce of all time in football. And we lost 1-0.

Middlesbrough is a big club and we were given the five-star treatment – never mind the four-star – the players were treated as ballerinas. When we travelled away we wouldn't go on the day, we'd go weeks beforehand! We found ourselves mid-table with two away games coming up: Swindon in midweek, then Swansea on the Saturday. If we'd lost those two games we'd have dropped into the lower reaches, which Middlesbrough couldn't accept. They needed at least two points out of these games (it was two points for a win then). They took us to Porthcawl for a week to cover the two games as they were relatively close. I went in to see the manager Raich Carter and asked if he minded if I took my wife down to Swansea then come back to the Seabank Hotel in Porthcawl. He said, "Mel, I don't want to be nasty but we're going away for points. It's costing the club a lot of money and I can't be making exceptions for different players." Okay, I accepted that, so I left my wife up in Middlesbrough and off we went to South Wales.

When we got to the Seabank, I found I was sharing a room with one of the rogues as usual. The club always did this because they knew as club captain I would be able to control the more errant players. After checking in I said, "Right, I'm off – I'm going to the pictures," and strode out of the hotel. I had to be a bit shifty as I wasn't going to the pictures, I was heading home to Swansea. I ran all the way from the seafront at Porthcawl to the A48. I didn't know how far it was, but I knew that I would probably be able to get a bus from there. I didn't think about a taxi; you just didn't in those days because you didn't have the money. (I'd never had a taxi in my life. We only had Glamtax in Swansea and besides, I used to run everywhere.)

I got a bus, but by the time I got back to Swansea time was rolling on. I had to be back in the hotel by 10.30 and I was 9.15 by the time I got to my mother's house. "Where's Tony?" I asked her. "I need a car fast." I didn't have time to do anything before I was back out and running down the street. Where was I going to go – run into town? Run back to Porthcawl? I didn't know what I was doing, but as I was running down into Brynhyfryd my brother was driving up the road. I stopped the car and as he opened the door I grabbed him, threw him on the floor and drove away! He didn't know what hit him. I drove back to Porthcawl and walked in whistling a tune. "Alright lads? Yeah, lovely. Great film."

Return to Vetch Field

Swindon had Don Rogers, Mike Summerbee, Ernie Hunt and Bobby Woodruff – a great team at that time, really going places. We got our two points thanks to a goal from Gordon Jones. After winning there, the attitude was that anything from the Swansea match would be a bonus. I can remember arriving at the Vetch to a lot of fuss, to friends and fans calling me all the names under the sun because I was coming back to play *against* the Swans.

As I led 'Boro out of the tunnel, Raich Carter turned to me as he was about to go to the dugout and said, "Mel, go centre-forward today, son. We've got the two points we came away for. Go up there and enjoy yourself." I said, "What are we going to do about centre-half, boss?" "Put Taffy in there," he said. It was just the opportunity I wanted. When Swansea Town sold me, Trevor Morris made a mistake by declaring in the press: "We've got a centre-half to replace Mel already." In effect he was comparing Mike Johnson to me. Now nobody likes that – I certainly didn't. I like Mike, he's a nice lad, but why go comparing us? The way he said it was wrong, especially after he'd sold me to Middlesbrough when I'd just bought a bloody house in Swansea!

Centre-forward and centre-half are much the same role. As a centre-half I knew what I wouldn't want the centre-forward to do. So if I go centre-forward I just do what I know the centre-half doesn't want me to do. Still following? You just reverse it. I ran at Mike Johnson and WHAM! I hit him up in the air, robbed him of the ball and laid one on for Jimmy Irvine who had only the keeper to beat. He nearly brought the old West Stand double-decker down with his shot. "Jimmy!" I shouted. "Sorry, Mel ..." He made up for that soon after by scoring, though the Swans quickly cancelled it out.

George Kirby was playing for Swansea at the time. He'd played for ten clubs because he was one of those players a club would get in if they were in difficulty towards the end of the season. He would get you out of trouble and keep you up. The laws of the game were so different then; you could tackle people hard, elbow people and hit goalkeepers into the net, that sort of thing. (You only have to show your studs to your opponent these days and you're sent off.) So George's tackling ability was advantageous at that time, shall we say. I used to hit back if I'd been tackled, but I would contain myself until the right time. That was very difficult to do, as players would normally show their feelings right away after they'd been tackled. I didn't show mine though, so they'd apologise to me. But they knew the first opportunity I had – WHAM! They'd be straight in the stand. I used to love that.

So it was one each and we had a corner, so George came back to mark me. That was his brief at corners; wherever I go he goes, even though he was centre-forward. By now Mike Johnson was staying away from me and I'd lost George as the ball came over. Swansea had a goalkeeper by the name of Ronnie Briggs, a Northern Ireland international who had come from Manchester United. He climbed in the air among the players, all six foot six of him, and grabbed the ball. Brilliant save. But as he came down he hit the ground and the ball came out of his hands. He was lying helpless on the ground as I came through the pack with my left peg. WHACK! Straight into the net!

Then I made a mistake. I instinctively ran to celebrate in front of the old East Bank, or the 'Town End' as it was known. It used to be packed in those days and they were right on top of the pitch. I could see the whites of their eyes before I realised the nastiness in their faces: "The *bastard!*" Swansea were at the bottom and badly needed the points, though they eventually did get relegated. I started back-tracking onto the pitch and I was gone! I was supposed to stay in Swansea after the match but I got straight on the coach and back to the North East. I couldn't have gone out that night; they would have lynched me ...

As much as I had enjoyed my time at Middlesbrough, I wanted to come back to Swansea. The problem was 'Boro wanted to recoup some of the money that they had paid for me and Swansea weren't in a position to buy me back. I could have gone to a lot of clubs, but decided I would go to the nearest club to Swansea. One day in training, I was called in to the manager's office where Raich Carter was with Danny Williams, manager of Swindon Town. "Mel, Danny is interested in taking you to Swindon. How do you feel about that?" Raich asked. "I've told you I don't want to go anywhere apart from Swansea!" I replied. "But Mel, they haven't got any money to take you back," he continued. Behind Raich's desk was a big map showing all the routes from the different football grounds. I noticed Swindon was there and Swansea was there and said, "Okay, looks like it's only up the road. I can walk home from Swindon." I didn't realise it was 150 miles. Relatively speaking, when you look at the map and see Middlesbrough, Swindon and Swansea, it didn't seem that far away.

While I was at Middlesbrough my wife was expecting our first child, Nicola. We had been in Swansea for about eight weeks during the close season. As soon as the whistle blew at the end of a season I would be back there as quickly as possible and spend the summer working on my properties. I left Marion in Swansea to have the baby because I wanted the child to be Welsh, and I went back up North to report for pre-season training. On your first day back they take your blood pressure and weigh you and so on. Most of the lads would have been on holiday and socialising and would have put weight on. I always went back lighter than the previous season because I'd been working all through the summer. Everyone else would be brown and I'd be white from working indoors all the time.

On the first day back I was just settling in when one of the young ground staff lads came in with a telegram for me. "Telegram?" I said. "Who's going to send *me* a telegram?" I opened it and it said: 'Baby girl, Rosemary.' It took me a little while to understand it. Who's Rosemary? Oh, that's my wife's sister. Right, it must mean Marion has had the baby. I'd only just put my football kit on but quickly got dressed again. I didn't tell the club, didn't ask anyone's permission, I just jumped in my car and sped out through the gates. All the players lined the road and cheered me off. I got back to the bungalow, picked up the poodle, Pepe, and put him in the car. I grabbed my case which was still unpacked from coming back up from Swansea a few days before, and I was in the car and gone.

A narrow escape

I was driving down the motorway, past the Doncaster by-pass, and came to a section where there were three lorries on the inside lane. I was cruising in the fast lane, doing about 80 or 90mph. I was flying along when suddenly the middle lorry of the three pulled into the fast lane right in front of me. He couldn't have looked in his mirror. It must have been a removal van, or something like that, because the tailboard of his wagon was down. I went straight under his tailboard and it went so close to the windscreen that it took the racing mirrors on my bonnet clean off. I swerved out and came off the motorway and down a steep embankment.

I flew down the bank screaming and straight onto the other motorway with the oncoming traffic, so I was flying along in the wrong direction. The momentum of the car, combined with my reflexes, shot the car back up the bank and I landed in a lay-by on the original motorway. I was soaking wet as though somebody had thrown a bucket of water over me, and with the shock of what had happened I was locked to the steering wheel. I was frozen and couldn't move my head or body. Other drivers who had seen what had happened were pulling up behind me and coming over and tapping on the window. I couldn't turn to speak. Once again I come back to being born lucky. It was a *miracle* how I came out of that alive.

When I eventually came around I carried on to Swansea, blowing my horn at all the lorries on the rest of the journey: "Get off the bloody road!" My wife was in Gorseinon Hospital and in those days they would keep the mother and child in for fourteen days. I went down there every day for ten days. I was only missing pre-season training and the club understood. They let Marion out early but I hadn't arranged somewhere for us to stay. I didn't want to trouble either of our families; I wanted to stay independent. So we would have to stay in a hotel, and this is where I was lucky once again. We jumped in the car and didn't know where we were going. We tried all the hotels on the seafront but they were all full, so we had to stay with my mother. But I remember standing by the arch on Oystermouth Road, looking at all the hotels and saying to myself, "Right, one day – I'll get you." I never forgot that, so from then on, whenever I was back in Swansea, I would drive along the front seeing if anywhere was for sale.

I still kept looking while I was playing for Swindon. I had bought a house in the centre of town, in Phillips Parade, but I always wanted somewhere on the front. I eventually bought number 252 after being told by a friend it was available. I was so excited to be getting somewhere on the seafront that I shook hands on the deal straight away – I didn't even bother to try and negotiate. I soon noticed that the owners of the neighbouring houses were taking people in for B&B. They began knocking on my door too, and I'd open it and say, "Can't you read?" I'd put a private sign on the front gate and a private residence sign on the front door, but they still kept knocking. I eventually said to my wife, "Why don't we try it? Let's give the guest house business a go." For three years we ran it as hotel and we were full every single night. The hotel business happened by accident, like my property business which started when I moved to Middlesbrough and rented out the house I had just bought in Swansea. I never planned any of it!

While I was at Middlesbrough, the Swans did

brilliantly in getting to the FA Cup semi-final in 1964. It was such a shame they didn't go all the way to the final. I knew all the boys, they were my team pretty much, with the exception of Mike Johnson who had replaced me. We didn't go far in the cup competitions at 'Boro, so it was ironic that within a couple of years of leaving Swansea they went on a fantastic run. Then, the year after I left Swindon to come back to Swansea, Swindon won the League Cup. I couldn't have been that good a player, could I?

Swindon skipper

When I left Middlesbrough I could have gone to Leeds, but that would have been pointless as I wanted to come home, and since Swansea couldn't afford me I ended up at Swindon Town. They brought a few players in and had a brilliant team: Rod Thomas, Peter Downs, Stan Anderson (not the Newcastle one) and John Trollope, as well as established players like Don Rogers, Ernie Hunt and Bobby Woodruff. Mike Summerbee had just gone to Manchester City but it was still a strong side, in the old Division Two.

I was still living in Middlesbrough when I made my Swindon debut at Hull City, so a few of my friends from 'Boro came with me. I hadn't met my new team-mates so I didn't know anyone's name, and when I cleared the ball it hit one of my fellow defenders and rebounded straight into the net. Despite that I was made captain and voted player of the year for the three seasons I was with them, by both the players and the fans. I remember having to open a new Tesco store while I was there! We were never challenging for promotion but we weren't struggling either – it was always middle of the table. That's not to say there weren't some memorable games.

Swindon's local derby was against Reading, and playing centre-forward for the Royals was Pat Terry. When I was on the ground staff down the Vetch, Swansea signed Pat from Newport County. As I mentioned, Pat couldn't half jump, and he could head the ball well, too. These were the days when you could really challenge with your shoulder, and Pat was very useful at this. Years had passed since we had played in the same team at Swansea and he found himself at Reading, playing under future Swans manager Roy Bentley. We were both captains so we met in the middle to toss the coin. We shook hands and greeted each other. "Alright, Pat?" "Hello, Mel!" The referee was Clive Thomas – 'Clive the Book' – from Porthcawl. It was the first time I had met him and he had a big Welsh dragon on his black jersey. I said, "Cor, it's lovely to see the Welsh flag flying!" but he took offence at that and looked at me so sternly that I wondered what I had done.

Knowing how good Pat was in the air, I went up for the first ball that came over and knocked him flying, winning the ball in the process. Clive Thomas was standing about ten metres away and called me over. I didn't feel I'd done anything wrong so I stood firm. I edged towards him and he gave me a warning: "You go near him again and you'll be off this pitch!" I know Clive now and we're best of friends but I was terrified of him back then. I was aware of Pat's ability and threat, but I was more aware of Clive's strictness. We ended the game in defeat by three goals to one as I was afraid to challenge Pat after that warning and he took advantage of the situation.

The Little Book

In our days, if somebody kicked you on the football pitch, whether it was deliberate or not, you would have to get them back. This also applied if someone hurt one of my players. Centre-halves had a little book and the names would go in with a mark alongside them. Big Jack Charlton certainly took note if somebody took the mickey. You didn't turn the other cheek in those days. So when we met Reading in the return match I knew I'd be marking Pat Terry once again. I pulled into the car park before the match and the Reading team bus was arriving at the same time. I saw Pat and we walked up to the entrance with an arm on each other's shoulder. I said, "Pat, I've been waiting a long time for this. It's a lovely day today and I'm going to enjoy myself." "Yes," he said, "it is lovely today isn't it, Mel." He didn't realise what I meant. Then, when Pat was on the ball and went to turn, I hit him right off the field and across the track. He grazed his side badly on the red ash track and the ref blew for a foul. "Sorry, Ref," I said. Pat said, "Jesus, Mel – *take your time!*" I apologised to him too but it was a false gesture. I hit him again and this time he cottoned on. "You *bastard*, now I know what you meant!" It became a real battle and he lost his cool. In turn the Swindon crowd turned on him and threw their cushions and programmes at him.

In front of the Main Stand, Pat put his foot on the ball and beckoned me to challenge him. I thought he was trying to drag me in before releasing the ball to a team-mate, but he didn't. He kept it and I went straight through him, stood all over him and walked away with the ball! For that alone the Swindon fans wanted to knight me. The tables turned and we won that game.

Within two months Swindon had signed Pat and we were best friends. He'd come down from London and had to pass my house to get to the County Ground. He used to come in and ask for a coffee as if he owned the place; that's how friendly we were. He was a great centre-forward and I believe he would be in today's game, too. He was one of the best headers of the ball I ever saw. If you ask Mel Charles or others from the time I think they would agree.

We went to Shrewsbury Town for a midweek game and the pitch at Gay Meadow was as lovely as it sounds. Our manager Danny Williams called the referee over before the game and asked if he could have a word. Shrewsbury had a centre-half by the name of Woods who had a bad reputation and our manager wanted the referee to keep his eye on him. In a game against Tranmere, Woods had tackled an opponent so hard he broke his ribs and punctured his lung – he nearly killed him. The lad never played again, so I was told. It meant nothing to me as he was centre-half up one end of the field and I was centre-half down the other end. But halfway through the game, after he'd been having a real dig at my forwards, he came up front because they were behind and he thought he could knock us about a bit. Suddenly there was a 50/50 challenge on the halfway line between him and me. BANG! I hit him really hard and walked straight through him, so he quickly returned to centre-half. My players tried to chair me off the field at the end.

When I left Swindon, they turned to Sunderland to replace me with Frank Burrows, a name that will be familiar to all Swans fans because many years later he was appointed Swansea City manager. After his appointment, and just prior to pre-season training commencing, Frank was doing a few days' running to get himself in shape. He was running up Oystermouth Road then stopped outside my hotel. I was sitting there on the bench with my wife and looked up. "Hello, Frank," I said. I didn't know him but was well aware of him. I don't know how he knew me, either, but he replied, "Hiya, Mel. When I went to Swindon they didn't half give me some stick. They were comparing me with you all the time. You must have been some ****ing player!" That was the last thing I expected from Frank, but I respected him for it. He had two spells at the Vetch but I wasn't involved with the club during either and I don't think I ever spoke to him again.

7

Back Home

I HAD ENJOYED MYSELF AT Swindon but after two and a half years I wanted to come home. The Swans didn't come in for me, but by 1968 I'd been away for seven years and I'd had enough.

As I stated earlier, I sent half of my wages from Middlesbrough back to Swansea and supplemented my income with a tri-weekly newspaper article. The money I'd been putting away had allowed me to purchase a few run-down properties in Swansea. Over the previous years, every time I'd been home I'd purchased a dilapidated house for reasonable money and worked on it so I could let it out while I was away playing football. Now my aim was to come back and dedicate myself to this business full-time.

A young Swans player called Giorgio Chinaglia was living in one of my flats with another youngster called Mike Hayes. Giorgio used to come down the Vetch scruffy and tired from partying all night. His parents were in Cardiff and he was enjoying his independence. He had ability but he wasn't working at it. Of course, he went on to become a superstar a decade later with New York Cosmos.

I got George Bros, the removals people, up to Swindon, shoved all my furniture onto the lorry and headed home. Unfortunately for me the vice-chairman of Swindon Town, Mr Green, was driving down the dual-carriageway near to where I lived and saw the removal van outside my house. He carried on to the County Ground, parked up and asked, "What's going on around at Mel's?" Nobody at the club had any idea what I was doing. I was coming back to Swansea lock, stock and barrel and they were none the wiser. They phoned my house and got no answer, so they phoned my mother who knew what I was planning and told them of my intentions. Once they realised I'd left Swindon and had no intention of coming back, they rang me every day through the summer months, saying, "Don't do anything silly – you're still a Swindon player." I said to Danny Williams, "Look Boss, I've got nothing against the club but I've come back to Swansea, and if I have to I'll finish with football completely."

I started working on my properties and was really enjoying it. I was so excited at coming home and doing what I wanted to do that it never entered my head to approach the Swans about a possible return. Billy Lucas was manager of Swansea Town at this time and he became aware I was back in the city. He came up to my mother's house in Carmarthen Road, Fforestfach, where I was staying with my wife until we sorted out a place for ourselves. He asked if I'd like to come back down the Vetch. I was still young – not yet 31 – so I said, "Of course I would." I wanted to concentrate on my business though, because I realised that was my future.

Changes

The Swans had gone down two divisions in the time I was away and were now in the old Fourth Division. Things had changed; when I left there had been a team full of internationals, but they had all gone. It was almost a different ball game. The club was at a low ebb, drawing crowds of 4,000. Seven years earlier it had been 20,000 upwards. I've got a photo on the wall in my hotel bar with all the players from my first spell with the Swans: Trevor Ford, Mel Charles, Ivor and Len Allchurch, Cliffy Jones, Terry Medwin, Roy Paul, and then me. The caption says: 'The last of the production line.' To be included with those players was brilliant. There are a lot who were left out, legends like Ray Daniel, Barrie Jones, Herbie Williams and Harry Griffiths. So Swansea Town – soon to become Swansea *City* – were a different proposition altogether in 1968.

The first training session was over in Port Talbot at the Afan Lido. I'd never been over there before. I didn't know many of the boys – Vic Gomersall, Alan Williams, Tony Millington, David Gwyther – though I did know Herbie and Geoff Thomas. They were on hard times but it was a tidy team. We had a game up at Workington and it turned out to be Billy Lucas' last game in charge. He had a secret plan to make a statement that things weren't going well at the club, but it backfired on him that day.

We'd been hammered by Workington at the Vetch the previous season. For this game, Billy took a team of kids with myself as one of only two senior players, along with a big, strong, experienced striker called Alfie Biggs. Then there were youngsters like Billy Screen, Clive Slattery and Carl Slee. I think Billy was expecting us to get another hammering with the team he had picked. I remember saying to Alfie, "Let's get out there and show 'em what we can do. You sort their defence out and I'll sort out their attack." He was knocking their defenders all over the park and in the first ten minutes their forward Kit Napier was taken off on a stretcher. We won 3-0! We were all pleased afterwards but then found out that Billy Lucas had resigned that morning and not told us. We didn't find out until we read it in the papers.

The following season Roy Bentley was brought in as manager, after a few years at Reading. An ex-England international, he had been a great player and was a true gentleman. We'd be training at the Vetch, doing corners and whatever, and he was in such good shape he'd be joining in, really driving them across at us. He'd played for Chelsea and Fulham and was a legend up there, with over 300 games for Chelsea, averaging a goal in every three. He was a good manager and he really organised things. Swansea didn't have the money to go out and bring players in; any newcomers would be from Llanelli or Merthyr or clubs like that. Harry Griffiths had been assistant to Billy Lucas and stayed on with Roy Bentley. The club wasn't big enough, or *thinking* big enough, to change. They were lucky to get a manager of any description because they were paying peanuts.

So it was much the same team for the 1969/70 season but it was more organised. They brought Lennie Allchurch back on one wing and we had Brian Evans on the other. They were both very good players. We also had Dai Gwyther and Herbie Williams up front, so the four of them were quality. Barrie Hole, Geoff Thomas and Alan Williams were in the middle of the park, Vic Gomersall at left-back, Dai Lawrence at right-back, and young Carl Slee. Tony Millington in goal was a natural comedian. We'd be trying to play football and he'd be entertaining the crowd – but *what* a goalkeeper! It was because Roy Bentley came in and organised us correctly that we achieved promotion to the old Third Division. With our blend of youth and experience we were a force for anybody.

Elland Road

In the FA Cup we were beating Leeds United up at Elland Road with ten minutes to go. All we had to do was see the game out. It was almost a formality. You couldn't get in Elland Road in those days, it was packed. The team they had – Norman Hunter, Jack Charlton, Mick Jones – was incredible. The Leeds forward Allan Clarke did what they all seem to do today but you didn't see back then: he went down on the floor holding his head and rolling around. I honestly didn't touch him. The referee was ten yards away and should have booked him for play-acting, but instead I was sent off. It was unfair. To prove the point the club insisted on a personal hearing. I pushed him away, I didn't hit him at all. If he's alive, which I hope he is, he'll tell you. The infamous Elland Road crowd got me sent off. There were forty-odd thousand shouting: "OFF! OFF! OFF!" The linesman was terrified and called over the ref, who came up to me and said, "I'm sorry Mel, but you've got to go." That's how he put it to me. He had actually seen what happened and should have overruled the linesman but he didn't. I walked off the field dejected. Brian Evans missed an open goal which would have finished it. No-one blamed Brian because he'd done well to get into that position. Leeds then threw everything at us and with a man advantage they scraped two goals.

The club appealed against my red card. David

Goldstone, the chairman, and myself went to a personal hearing with the Football Association at a hotel in Birmingham. At that same hearing were Liverpool's Tony Hateley and Emlyn Hughes, accompanied by their manager Bill Shankly. I knew Shanks to say hello to as I'd played against his Liverpool team. There was another lad there from Bristol Rovers, though his name escapes me. We were all waiting outside to have our appeals heard.

David Goldstone was a solicitor and he insisted on representing me. He told me beforehand: "Don't speak during the hearing, Mel. Don't say a thing – just leave it to me." The panel we were facing was made up of five people, all ex-footballers. I didn't even want to appeal. I'd been sent off, we'd lost the bloody game and that was that as far as I was concerned. Whatever the outcome of the hearing you can't go back, can you? I shouldn't have been sent off but I had been, and now it was gone.

David Goldstone was treating it as though he was in a court of law; he even had his barrister's tie on. It felt like I was staring at a life sentence, so I spoke up. Mr Goldstone didn't like it but I had to as I was on the same level as these ex-players and I knew how to put my case across better. The referee and linesman from the game were also present. "Gentlemen," I began, "I've been playing this game a long time now and I've played under this gentleman, the referee, many times before and I've always found him to be fair and honest." The referee then spoke up on my behalf: "Yes, I've refereed many games that Mel has played in and he's always been fair and above board." Well, this testimonial was better than any barrister in the land. Bang – £20 fine and no suspension. If I had left it to Mr Goldstone they would have fined me heavily and banned me for a month! It worked out fine and both of us travelled back to Swansea happy. Likewise, Bill Shankly, being a real football person, got Hateley and Hughes off their charges.

Simple economics

Not long after this I finished playing football because I couldn't afford to continue. Because the club had so many young players, Roy Bentley announced he wanted us back in the afternoon for training. He didn't want the youngsters on the streets, hanging around the betting shops or snooker rooms, or whatever it was they did with time on their hands. This was fine for them but I couldn't accept it. I could have done that at Middlesbrough or Swindon but I'd left those two great clubs to come back and run my business. I felt I'd sacrificed my mornings to train, and if we were playing away I'd sacrifice whole weekends, although I accepted that and just got on with it. I'd expected to have my afternoons off. I had enjoyed a couple of seasons back with the Swans but I was at a crossroads. So I left at the end of that promotion season and the club accepted that.

I wanted to play football but it wasn't practical; I could have played three or four more years but then what? I wasn't going into football management. Although I thought I would be capable of it, I didn't want to because you have to depend on other people and I don't like that. As a player it's down to you: you determine your own future by how you apply yourself in training, how you look after yourself, and subsequently how you perform on the pitch. So I felt management or coaching would be a nightmare.

At this time I was in town and walking down Union Street when I bumped into a young lad called Dougie Rosser who had just been invited to sign professional forms for the club. He was at the age where he was learning a trade, but the club thought he was good enough to make the grade – which he did as he was a good player. Doug didn't know which way to turn; should he sacrifice his trade for football or sacrifice football for his trade? The reality was that he would be earning less playing football. He wanted my opinion on what he should do, centre-half to centre-half. My advice was, "Look, Doug, I know football is a very short life but if I were you I'd sign professional now as you won't have this chance again, whereas you will have the opportunity to pick up your trade again if things don't work out on the football pitch." Based on that, Dougie did sign professional, and being a fit, strong lad he did well. He came on at Elland Road when I got sent off against Leeds and played for the first team. In fact the only problem he had in getting picked was that I was still there! I'm joking, of course, but this is an example of the dilemmas players faced in those days as there was no money in the game.

At the start of the following season, 1970/71, I was happy working on my houses. The Swans weren't so happy, with two points from their first eight games. It was ridiculous; they'd gone up a division and the only player out of the team was myself, but they kept on losing. Well, I couldn't go anywhere in Swansea because everyone was blaming me! I'd sit outside my hotel on the benches and cars would go past blowing the horn with people waving their fists at me, shouting, "You swine!" – among other things. I didn't know what to do.

I was still going down the Vetch to watch the games but I'd try and go in disguise.

This is where Roy Bentley was wrong: he should have realised that the senior players, like myself, had business interests outside the game. Barrie Hole ran a newsagents, Len Allchurch was in the shoes and clothes game, and the manager should have made allowances for these players. These guys weren't going up the ladder now, they were coming *down* and having to think about life after football. But he said, "Everybody comes back in the afternoon."

I hadn't fallen out with anybody at the club. I bought a house and one of the directors helped me negotiate for it, so I felt I owed him. One game I was sneaking in with the crowd, trying not to be noticed, when I saw this director making a bee-line for me. I looked up at him and said, "Okay, I'll go and offer my services tomorrow." He stopped in his tracks, didn't say a word and turned around.

The following day I phoned up the club and spoke to the secretary Gordon Daniels, making an appointment to see the manager. I went to see him in the boardroom at the Vetch, which most Swans fans will remember as the Harry Griffiths Bar, as it would become some years later. Bang on 10 o'clock I was knocking on the door. No answer. This went on for five minutes, then ten. I thought, "I've come down here to offer my services and they can't even keep the appointment." I didn't even *want* to come back! Anyway, I turned around and got about fifty yards away from the Vetch when the door opened and Gordon called me back. Whether this was deliberate I don't know, but they kept me waiting again inside.

MEL
NURSE

Cwmbwrla Boys Football Team, 1948/49. That's me holding the ball.

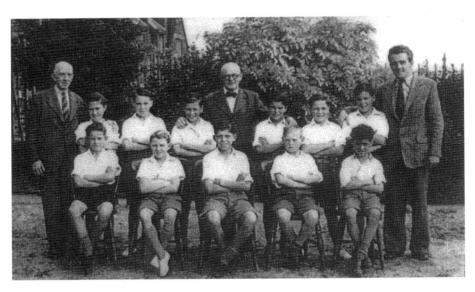

Nurse at the crease. Cricket for Cwmbwrla in 1949.

Early days in my beloved white shirt. Standing, third left.

Making my debut for Swansea, March 1956, in front of a packed North Bank.

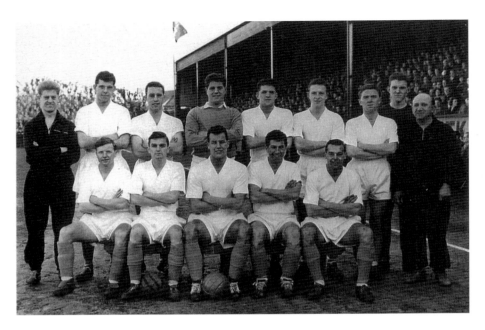

Lining up for Swansea Town's first team 1958/59 with Mel Charles as Skipper.

Proudly wearing the Swans shirt with fellow defenders Brian Hughes and Malcolm Kennedy.

My last season with Swansea Town, 1961/62

Playing for my country. Always a very proud moment.

Facing Di Stefano in Madrid with Wales, May 1961.

Signing for Middlesborough in 1962, watched by Bob Dennison and Harry Green.

Smiling despite not being in Swansea! My time at Middlesborough.

My Swindon Town days.

Back home. Rejoining the Swans in 1968.

LEEDS SCRAPE IN AFTER NURSE IS SENT OFF

Leeds 2, Swansea 1: By JOE CUMMINGS

SWANSEA will long be remembered by Yorkshire folk as the Soccer small fry who teased, tormented and almost "fried" the big fish of Leeds.

They had the League champions dangling on a hook for an agonising seventy minutes. And this despite losing their biggest hero, Mel Nurse, after ten minutes of the second half.

He was sent off following a clash with £150,000 Allan Clarke. The Leeds striker's boot landed in Nurse's stomach and Clarke ended up on the floor.

What a pity! It will always be questioned whether Leeds would have won had that not happened. Nurse was the goalmouth guardian that the Champions, with all that talent, could not remove.

Only when he had gone could Leeds find a path to goal. It left them with a very hollow victory — an insipid success that went close to being a total humiliation.

STEADY

When Nurse was there Swansea were never over-awed by the high-ranking opposition. Only in the first five minutes did they look tentative and likely to succumb.

A great ball from Norman Hunter sent Mick Jones away on the left wing and his hard, low centre was almost turned into his own net by full back Vic Gomersall.

But the Welshmen showed their resilience with three quick counter-punching attacks.

David Gwyther broke clear, but mis-kicked when he reached the Leeds penalty area.

Four minutes after that, Herbie Williams lashed the ball only inches wide.

And so it went on. Leeds looked insecure and their distribution was atrocious at times

CASUAL

When the chances came, they missed them in amateurish fashion. Clarke had three opportunities and squandered them all.

Swansea found each other with precise passes as they attacked with determination and guile.

It paid off in the twenty-fourth minute, when Brian Evans thumped in a fierce shot which Sprake could only palm away and Gwyther was there to jab it into the net.

What a turn-up! It threw Leeds into such dithering insecurity that, had Swansea taken their chances, they could have had two more goals before half-time.

With Nurse's departure only heroic work by goalkeeper Tony Millington and his defenders kept Leeds out.

In the seventieth minute Lawrence handled the ball in a goalmouth scramble and Giles coolly slotted home the equaliser.

Ten minutes later Jones met a corner-kick from Peter Lorimer to head the winner.

Newspaper report of my dismissal at Leeds. I should never have been sent off.

In action during my second spell with the Swans.

Celebrating promotion to Division Three, 1970. Chairman David Goldstone in the foreground.

My last days at the Vetch Field as a player, 1971. With Dai Gwyther, Geoff Thomas, Roy Bentley and Herbie Williams.

With some legends of Swansea Town/City at a function, late 1980s.

With Mel and John Charles in my hotel, early 2000s.

Accepting the lifetime achievement award from Huw Cooze, Liberty Stadium, April 2009.

Boots back on!

Eventually I was sat around the big table in the boardroom with the manager Roy Bentley and the chairman David Goldstone, who was a very wealthy man. For the next twenty minutes I just sat there listening to the pair of them talking about me as if I wasn't there. "Shall we take a chance and sign him on?" "Is he good enough to get in the team?" "Is he fit enough?" and so on. I couldn't believe it – and it went on for so long that I stood up and said, "Gentlemen, I'm very sorry but I'm obviously wasting your time. I thought I was helping the situation but I can see I'm not." I went to walk away and the chairman said, "Mel, hang on. I'll tell you what: there's a contract there – sign it and we'll take a chance on you ... Of course, you sign it for appearance money only." Now appearance money, as you can imagine, means if you're not in the first team you don't get paid. They wanted me to do everything a professional footballer does: train every morning and travel away, and when they wanted to play me they would. I said, "Look, Mr Chairman, the last contract I had with you was for £20 a week, not appearance money. Now, I'll sign that same contract and whether you play me is up to you. I'm not doing this for my benefit; you need a bit of help and I'm willing to help but I won't sign a contract for anything less." The moment I signed the contract Mr Goldstone announced, "Right, you're playing Saturday." Talk about wily.

Roy Bentley, the actual team manager, told Mr Goldstone to hang on. He had doubts about my match fitness, and he was right. I was fit, but not match fit. When you have trained all your life you can't just stop dead. So every night I was working in my hotel on Oystermouth Road, in the shadow of the Vetch, I'd run up to Blackpill and back at about eight or nine o'clock. Roy Bentley believed I needed four weeks to get match fit so he didn't select me for the next game. He put me in the reserves and my first game was against Cardiff City at Ninian Park. They announced that I was coming back from retirement and as I ran out onto the pitch in front of a crowd of about 2,000, everybody clapped me onto the field. Can you imagine Cardiff people clapping a Swansea player onto the field?

I've played against Cardiff many times and we used to vent our feelings on the field. We'd criticise each other and have a bit of fun. Any problems that had to be solved were sorted out on the pitch. The supporters used to mingle among themselves; there was no such thing as segregation, they were all as one, and these were full houses, remember. It was a wonderful atmosphere.

There's nothing wrong with Cardiff, let me say that. If they had come for me and asked me to play for them, I would have. I don't know what's gone wrong with society. Look at the 2008/09 season: when Swansea and Cardiff got to the fourth round of the FA Cup there was speculation, premature as it turned out, that they could meet. People were hoping that if Cardiff went through then Swansea wouldn't get drawn against them, because of all the crowd trouble there would inevitably be. I just can't understand that attitude. It's getting out of hand now, and the minority are spoiling it for the majority. I don't know how to stem that. I want Cardiff to achieve, not over us obviously, but good luck to them apart from that. *We're all Welsh.*

Anyway, on this particular day, up front for Cardiff

reserves were two big fellows – Brian Clark and Derek Showers. I had a load of kids around me because the senior players were in the first team. Roy Bentley was right: I wasn't match fit, so I spent the game talking to Clarky and Showers, just passing the time of the day. I didn't want them going out wide; they'd have run me into the ground! Cardiff had a trainer by the name of Wilf Grant and he realised what was happening. He was out of the dugout, running down the track and shouting at them to ignore me. Clarky said, "What's *he* on about?" and I said, "Don't worry about him. How's life?" We beat them 1-0. If they'd listened to Wilfie, they'd have been running all over the place and half killed me!

I spent a few more weeks in the reserves before getting back into the first team. Though the Swans were still on the slide, we pulled ourselves together. My first game was away at Tranmere. They used to have their floodlights on the roof of the stands, so when the goalie kicked the ball high up in the sky it would disappear. You'd position yourself where you thought it would come down. Can you imagine it? It would come back down and smack you on the head!

Another sign that I wasn't fully match fit was that I did my usual amount of talking on the pitch but lost my voice. When I was on the field I used to shout a lot. I don't see that happening so much now. You don't see captains really pushing people around; they toss the coin and represent the club off the field. A captain's role was far different forty-odd years ago, it seems. Anyway, all the way back from Tranmere on the coach I couldn't speak a word.

Liverpool in the Cup

In my final season, 1970/71, we met Liverpool at Anfield in the FA Cup. What a draw. It was very good for the club financially. Before the game we were sitting in the dressing room and everyone was there: the players, management and directors, our entire party. The chairman Mr Goldstone said he wanted everybody out of there except the players and manager. "Lads, on behalf of the club," he said, "I'd like to thank you all for your efforts as this Cup run has helped keep the club afloat. You've done a fantastic job so we thank you very much." Now, I was just about to finish my career and, while I respected the chairman as a person, I couldn't care really, so as he turned around I said, " ... and there's me thinking you were about to give us something for getting so far!" Mr Goldstone knew it was me who said it as he recognised the voice. He turned around and gave me the sort of look that suggested he'd have shot me if he'd had a gun. I knew that we were on our usual £4 a man to win, by way of a bonus, and that Liverpool were on far, far more than that. I was just speaking my mind but he didn't see the funny side of it.

We lost the game itself 0-3 and I was sick as we'd held them for so long. John Toshack was playing for Liverpool and he was a big, strong lad who was very good in the air. Ian Callaghan, another who would go on to play for Swansea some eight years later, went down the line and Carl Slee went out to him and brought him down. Carl then picked up the ball and gave it to Cally for the free kick, who promptly put it down and crossed it. I had gone to support Carl as I planned to nail Cally if he got past him. So by the time I ran back to the far post the ball had come over and Tosh had put it away.

Nothing Tony Millington could do about it. Once they had scored our heads dropped and they were in full flight – in fact if the game had gone on they might have scored 23, not three.

I came off the field covered in mud and sat in the corner of the dressing room absolutely gutted. Len Allchurch, Barrie Hole – we were all gutted with our heads down. We couldn't believe we'd lost 0-3 as we were in with a chance for much of the game. I took my boots off and threw them down. Mr Goldstone and his Liverpool counterpart, Mr Anderson if I remember rightly, came into the dressing room. The Liverpool chairman asked, "Which one of you is Nurse?" I put my hand up as if I was in school. "Me, sir." He said, "If you carry on playing like that, son, you'll play until you're 100." I got away with what I'd said earlier to Mr Goldstone when he heard that. Not that I was worried about it.

The contract I'd signed in front of Mr Goldstone and Roy Bentley was to get the club out of trouble. Once Swansea City couldn't get relegated, I was walking away. I'd signed on that premise. Then we started winning games and suddenly found ourselves about sixth in the table. They then start talking about promotion! The rest of the players didn't know about the unusual contract I had with the club so were very shocked when, after training at the Vetch one morning, I announced I was done. I went to tell Roy Bentley I was off and this time I wouldn't be coming back. I told him while he was still in the bath. "Rubbish," he said, "you can't just walk out like that!" I reminded him of the contract and that I could do whatever I wanted to do. I walked out of his little bathroom and out of the Vetch.

I was walking down Glamorgan Street and Roy came chasing after me with a towel wrapped around him. I can see it now! He said, "Mel, you can't finish just like that. You know the reserve team centre-half has had a knock. You can't leave me in the lurch." I knew this was true about Doug Rosser, the second team centre-half, so I said, "Okay, based on that I'll train the rest of the week and play Saturday." We beat Chesterfield 1-0 in the mud, courtesy of a Dai Gwyther goal, and afterwards I threw my boots down and said, "Right, that's it – I'm finished!" I was summoned to the boardroom and didn't half take some stick, but I told them I'd honoured the contract I'd signed and I was free to go.

I had played my last game for the Swans.

Into the Valleys

Within a couple of weeks of quitting the game I was approached by a gentleman called Des Shankley who was running Pembroke Borough in the Welsh League. I knew Des from before and he would always say, "When you finish playing for Swansea, Mel, come down and have a game for us." I went down to West Wales and played for them for a couple of months before a nasty outbreak of shingles, which lasted a few months, finished my Pembroke career. As I was getting over the shingles, I was back working in my hotel when who should walk through the door but John Charles. "You fit?" he asked. "Yes," I said, "why do you ask?" He said, "Would you like to come up and have a game for me?"

'Big John' was player-manager of Merthyr Tydfil who had some good players. All the clubs around there fed off the Swans, Cardiff and Newport, with lots of decent ex-professionals turning out. He didn't want to talk about money, he just said he'd give me what he was giving the other lads which was £20 a game. I'd been earning £20 a week at Swansea, so if I played two games for Merthyr in a week I was getting twice as much. Not that I was concerned about the money. I still wanted to play and I realised I didn't want to finish just like that, as I had done at the Swans. It was a good compromise because I could play amateur for Merthyr and run my business, so I stayed with them for three years.

When I was playing for Merthyr, if there was a free kick around the halfway line, I would have to go up to take it. We won most of our games from John Charles heading the ball, so it was down to me to put it where he wanted it. If somebody else was going to kick it, he'd bark, "*Leave it!* Mel?"

One day when we were at Penydarren Park, the ball was in play and I was trying to put it in the air for John to get his head to. As I connected with the ball, this lad came in on my blindside with six studs up and snapped my leg. I lay on the floor, holding my leg above the knee and trying to stop the pain coming up it. The other lad was also on the floor and I was concerned he had broken his leg. I'd heard the impact but, although I was in pain, I didn't believe my leg could have broken because I had big, strong legs. I closed my eyes momentarily and when I opened them again the other lad was gone. Then I saw his legs dangling about a metre above me. John had seen what had happened, sprinted down the field, picked him up by his neck and was shaking him like a rag doll.

I still didn't think there was anything badly wrong as my leg wasn't out of shape. They pulled me up and as soon as I put my foot back down I said, "Take me off." I knew then that there was some serious damage, so Frank Hegarty, the coach, took me down to the Prince Charles Hospital. I was waiting in the foyer, still in my Merthyr kit, with a couple of lads either side of me who were both saying they had broken legs too and were practically crying with the pain. I was hoping mine wasn't broken and said I thought it was just hurt.

Suddenly the swing-doors flew open, a trolley came through and was rushed through the next set of swing-doors. What a sight – you couldn't tell if it was a man or a woman. Whoever it was had been travelling along the notorious Heads of the Valleys road when a lorry had come off a site onto the main road. A brick that had lodged behind one of its back wheels had flown straight through the windscreen and hit the driver of the car. Well, when I saw this I tried to pick my leg up and hobble out, as it put my injury into perspective.

Eventually the two other lads were seen. They came out bandaged up and left – nothing wrong with them. I got x-rayed and discovered my leg was broken in two places. They were plastering my leg up and the specialist, who also worked for Merthyr Tydfil FC, said, "Mel, do me a favour when you go back up the ground – have a word with the big fella because he's wrecking the place. He's knocking the place down up there!" John Charles had gone mad back at Penydarren Park. Two of the stewards – big lads, both ex-miners – were stopping John going in to the visitors' dressing room. He was trying to get in there to have a go at the fella who had broken my leg. Big John rammed them against the wall and put them both in hospital as well! He was causing murders up there.

Talking of injuries, I broke my nose three times on the football pitch too. It came with the territory in those days. Centre-halves would stick their heads in anywhere. Goalkeepers would come out to punch the ball and very often they'd miss.

I didn't think I'd play football again after breaking my leg, but after a few months out I was able to play again for Merthyr. There were five lads from Swansea – Mickey Lennon, Donnie Payne, Doug Rosser, Dai Jones and myself – turning out for Merthyr in the Southern League and we'd all travel up in my car. John Charles was player-manager for the club but he also had something to do with BP, like an ambassador or something, with a chauffeur-driven car. The three years we were together up at Merthyr he'd come to my hotel most days and drink all my whisky. I didn't drink but we'd sit and discuss what we were going to do on the Saturday. He loved his whisky but he could hold it.

I explained to John that I wanted my petrol covered for the journeys up to the Valleys and back and he said I could have £2 petrol money for each game. I'd leave it for five or six games then go into the office to collect the £10 or whatever. The boardroom at Penydarren Park was actually in the boiler room; they had a social club but the directors used to sit around a table in the tiny boiler room with big water tanks for company. I went in to collect what I was owed and the mood was a bit sombre. They said, "Mel, we're finding it very difficult at the moment ..." and before he was finished I'd shaken everyone's hand and was out of there. I was finished, just over the principle of it. John went wild but I'd made my mind up.

John continued to call by the hotel and one day he

told me he'd been offered a role as assistant to Harry Gregg at Swansea City. He asked me what I thought. "I think it's brilliant, John," I said. "I know they idolise you at Merthyr but this is a progression for you – the Swans are a league club." With his knowledge of football, the club had to benefit from it too, so it seemed like a good arrangement all round. He wasn't even forty years old at this stage, still a young bloke, and this was a good climb up the ladder. He relinquished his role at Penydarren Park and went down the Vetch. I went around there one day and John was painting the toilets. "What are you doing?" I asked. "Helping out," he said. I said, "John, you know when you asked me if you should go and be assistant manager down the Vetch? Well, the assistant manager doesn't paint the toilets!" I couldn't believe it. He had old shorts and old gym shoes on and was painting away, half-soaked – one of the most famous players in world football.

The next thing I knew, Merthyr came knocking, asking if I'd step into John's shoes up there. I think they thought I'd engineered John going down the Vetch so I could replace him, but nothing could be further from the truth. I didn't want to do it. They invited me to a dinner but I made it perfectly clear I had no intention of becoming involved in football management, at Merthyr or anywhere. My wife and I went up to the dinner and Eddie Thomas was there, the boxing trainer, and Ken Tucker the secretary. They tried to talk me in to taking on the role but I stood firm. They then appointed Les Graham as manager, from Newport County. It wasn't a good appointment and they lost a lot of matches. Soon they released Les.

They came back down to see me, through the back

door this time. "Will you help us out, Mel?" they asked. Now that's a different approach: they weren't asking me to become manager, they were just asking me to help them out of trouble. I don't want to see anybody in trouble so I agreed to go up there and see what I could do. I soon found myself getting involved in the development of the ground and with the players as I felt my name was at stake because I'd thrown my lot in with the club. I didn't take a penny off them and pretty soon I started to enjoy my involvement with Merthyr Tydfil, if I'm honest.

Merthyr are struggling to survive at the moment and seeing the coverage on the news recently has brought back memories of my time there. I hope they survive but it's going to be very difficult for them. All the workforce has gone up there, all the mines closed down long ago and Hoover has gone now as well. Times are hard and you just can't see how Merthyr are going to get through this. It's frightening.

Jack of all trades

In the early 1970s the Merthyr public took to me and it was working out well for all parties. One day I came out of the social club and saw one of the players going to see the chairman. I stood by my car and watched him, then called him over and put him on the spot. "Is the chairman giving you money behind my back?" I asked. It turned out he was and I couldn't put up with that. I told him to wait there and went straight to see Ken Tucker, who was known as 'Mr Merthyr' at the time as he worked tremendously hard for the club. I said, "Ken, I want to become a director of this club." I was paying out for a lot of things and thought I should really be on the board.

He called a meeting and everyone voted me on the board. So now I wasn't only the player-manager but a director as well. They'd only just voted me on when I said, "The first thing I'd like to do is make a vote of no confidence in the chairman, because he's undermining the manager by giving players money outside of what's been agreed." They put it to the vote and they all voted the chairman out. I was sitting there looking at them, then suddenly they were all looking to me. In that one meeting I went from being caretaker player-manager, to director, to chairman of Merthyr Tydfil Football Club. I'd only gone up there to help them out!

I bought them a minibus, took it in to Harry Guard in Swansea and had it sprayed black and white, put 'Merthyr Tydfil FC' on it, then converted it from a 12- to a 16-seater. It saved the club a lot of expenditure. I altered the ground and changed the social club to create a proper boardroom within it. I was selecting the team and playing when I was needed. I preferred to pick the young lads but would turn out whenever necessary. We had a big cup game coming up and, realising we were playing against a superior side from the Football League, I ordered extra training prior to the match. It was likely they would hammer us 6-0 or something so I hired the leisure centre in Merthyr and put them through their paces. It was also to show the people of the town that we were taking it seriously.

I was driving on the outskirts of Merthyr back to Penydarren Park and it was very dark. In those days they had small street lamps about 300 yards apart so it was dark between the lights. I wasn't travelling fast but an elderly lady stepped out in front of me. I was literally crawling along but she came out of the dark and into the path of the car. I got out and it was pelting down with rain. I didn't know what I'd hit – I thought maybe I'd hit a horse and it had run off. When I walked around the car I saw the elderly lady on the floor. I won't go into detail about it, but in the months after I lost two stone in weight from worry. The poor woman didn't make it and I felt terrible about it.

One of the directors at the club was an undertaker by the name of Jack James. He could see how wrought with worry I was and said, "Mel, I speak with the family regularly and they don't hold it against you. They're not blaming you." It was all well and good Jack saying that but it had happened. I finished with Merthyr immediately; I left everything and didn't go back there. Even to this day if I go up to Merthyr I won't travel down that road; I go the Cardiff way. The upset dragged on and on and I still think about it today. I went back to working on my properties and forgot about football.

8

Who *Me?*

I'D TURNED 40, PACKED in football and was going up to town to the bank in my working gear. Sam Jones was the manager of Lloyds Bank on Oxford Street at the time and I was up in his office discussing something. We were looking out the window up towards the Kingsway, watching all the people coming out of the Kardomah Café. I saw somebody come out and said to Sam, "Cor, look at him, he's done well – mohair suit, driving a Mercedes – good luck to him." I didn't *envy* him; I always think it's great to see people progressing. Sam turned to me and said, "When are you retiring, Mel?" I couldn't believe it. "What are you on about, Sam? I haven't bloody started yet, boy!" He said, "Well, what are you aiming for in life?" To which I replied, "Well there's two things, but I'll never achieve them. The first is a Rolls-Royce ..." "Well, why don't you go and get one?" he said. "Mr Jones, are you taking the piss out of me?" I laughed.

When I was small I can remember sitting on a bench with my brother waiting for a bus to come and I'd say to him, "The next thing to come along, kid, is yours." Somebody would come along on a bike and you'd think, "He must be wealthy!" Just to own a bike! You'd very rarely see a car on the road when I was young, so a Rolls-Royce was the ultimate.

Sam continued, "No, if you want one, go and get one." This was my bank manager telling me this! Then he said, "What's the second thing?" So I told him: "I'd love to be a director down the Vetch, but you have to be a billionaire to do that." In my day you used to see the directors and it was all yes-sir no-sir, you used to bow to them almost. They were moneyed people; beyond. I put them on a pedestal and I still do because the involvement, time, effort and finances they put in, the public don't see. People really don't realise. They take some stick, but when the club is failing they are laying out money right and left which isn't fair. Initially they should be spending, to get into that position and to show good faith, but then the club should run itself. But of course in the lower divisions it doesn't work like that.

So Sam said, "Well have you tried?" I'm like, "What do you mean, *tried?*" I couldn't believe what he'd just told me about the Rolls, never mind anything else. "Do you honestly think I'm in a position to become a director down the Vetch?" I asked. He said, "Well, I know Malcolm Struel, the chairman, and a couple of the directors. I'll have a word with them if you like." I came out of his office, out of the bank – I forgot what I'd gone in there for – and ran home. I left my van in town!

The next dream

I phoned Gordon Daniels, the club secretary at the time. "Oh, hello Gordon, can I make an appointment to see Mr Struel, please?" He said, "What about, Mel?" "Never mind what it's about. Please, just make an appointment for me to see him. I'd like to talk to Mr Struel." I always called Malcolm that as a sign of respect. He was a qualified solicitor and an absolutely fanatical supporter of the club. He was brilliant for the Swans, despite what some people may think. Eventually I went to see him.

Now just think about this: the one thing you want most in your life – how do you dress and how do you approach the situation? I didn't know. I didn't want to put a suit on because I thought it was too much, but I didn't want to go like a tramp in my working gear. So I eventually settled on a T-shirt and tidy trousers. I knew Malcolm from when I was playing as he was the chairman then, but I didn't know him on this level. So I went in and we spoke for a few hours about different things. He told me to go away and put what I was proposing in writing, then he in turn would present it to the board of directors at the next meeting.

In writing? I'm not clerically-minded at all, that's just not me. I'm not one for words, I'm more a practical person, so I didn't know how to word it. I wrote it, read it back, threw it away – this went on and on. In the end I broke it down into categories. With regards to the finance, again I didn't have a clue what to write. I didn't know what the finances of the club or the individual directors were – why would I? So what did I put? 'FINANCE: I WILL MEET ANY COMMITMENT OF ANY DIRECTOR.' Oh God. It could be £5,000 or it could be £500,000. It was open-ended! I didn't have a clue but I didn't want to ask anybody. I wanted to do it honestly and not go in the back door or anything. Keep it above board, if you'll pardon the pun.

I gave it in to the club. In their next meeting they had two things on the agenda. The first was for John Toshack to become player/manager; the other was my application to become a director. Now I understood the importance of John's application over mine – I'm not stupid. So I can imagine all the discussion in that boardroom and all the excitement was about John. The only thing I resent about it was that they didn't reply to me with regards to my application. They should have at least written back and explained: "Sorry Mel, we spent so much time on John that we didn't discuss you and we're putting it on hold for the moment." It was three months later when by chance I bumped into one of the directors, Winston Rees, in town and he put me in the picture.

John Toshack took over from Harry Griffiths in March 1978, though Harry stayed on to work with Toshy. Harry died just weeks later and it was both unexpected and sudden. He was still a young man, in his forties. He was a real Swansea person and had never shown an interest in leaving the city from what I can gather. As a footballer, he was the kind of player that I would want in my team if I was a manager. His attitude was right, he could climb and head the ball, he could play anywhere. In fact he had all the attributes of a true professional. Harry was thrown in at the deep end. He was a trainer at the Vetch, enjoying what he was doing, and I don't think he ever pushed himself forward for the manager's job in 1975. He just happened to be there so he accepted the responsibility and was fortunate at the time that there were some good young players coming through – Alan Curtis, Robbie James, Jeremy Charles. So that helped.

I had finished my playing career on a high, winning promotion with the Swans, and I felt I'd done everything that was asked of me by the club. Now I was president of the Swansea Schoolboys Association and also president of Treboeth FC. I would support both by organising fund-raising dinners and supplying kits and footballs, things like that. I couldn't give my time coaching, as they would have liked me to, but I'd help them financially. I had a hotel to run and a property business so I didn't have time to help out on the coaching front.

Tosh

Around about 1980 we had a dinner coming up for Treboeth Football Club and I was trying to get something a bit special to raffle. Tosh's team was going up through the divisions and the crowds down the Vetch had gone up from 3,000 to over 15,000. You couldn't get a season ticket without buying bonds first. The public in Swansea were on a high; the situation was very similar to what we experienced with Roberto Martinez. What Tosh did was brilliant, but I can never forgive him for what he did to me one day in the early years of his Swans career.

I had got a proper leather football, not an imitation one, and thought I'd get the Swans team to sign it for this dinner for Treboeth. Robbie James and Alan Curtis were idolised at the time. I knew them all from playing in charity matches, so I went down to the Vetch to get them to sign it. I was working on a house in the Sandfields and went down there about ten o'clock. Pat Abramson was working down there at the time and I said, "Pat, where are all the lads?" He replied, "They're down Ashleigh Road, Mel. John's got them down there and he could keep them on until one or two o'clock, you never know." Now, I couldn't afford to come away and miss them, because the dinner was that same night. So I stuck around, walking about the place not knowing what to do with myself. About one o'clock the players arrived. I shook hands with them, but before I got them to sign the ball I wanted to see Tosh and get his permission first – do it properly, out of respect. So I waited and waited and thought perhaps he'd come in the other gates. Then he walked up the old players' entrance from Glamorgan Street.

I said, "John, do you mind if I get this ball signed by the players?" I wasn't sure whether or not he heard me, but he walked up the tunnel and straight past me. It's only about five feet wide so you couldn't exactly miss me – I was filling half of it. But he just walked past and didn't acknowledge me at all. I thought, maybe he's miles away and he hasn't seen me, so I said, *"Jo-ohn?"* I shouted it before I realised he *had* heard me, but was ignoring me. Well, I couldn't accept that. The language I used I won't repeat in a family book, but if he'd turned around I'd have been tempted to welt him one! I was fuming.

Fortunately for me, as I'm shouting and swearing at him, Terry Medwin, who was his assistant, came through the gates. "Mel, what's going on? What's all the racket?" he asked. I said, "Terry, what an arrogant *******!" He said, "What are you after, Mel?" I explained all I wanted was the football signed. Christ, I could have gone in and got it done without asking him. He said, "Give it to me, I'll get it signed for you and I'll drop it in the hotel." I said, "Terry, *thank you*." Terry was as good as his word, but I never forgave John for that. I can't believe he did what he did. I speak to him now when I see him at the Liberty Stadium as I don't like to argue with people, but I won't be a doormat for anybody.

Cloughie

Talking of dinners, there was another one to celebrate Swansea City winning promotion to the First Division in 1981. The main guest speaker was to be Brian Clough. Peter Luprini, the owner of the Kardomah Café, was on at me about this dinner and asked if I'd go with him to hear Cloughie. (Peter and I had got to know each other as he lived in Llangenith and I was in Penclawdd. He always came over and sat with me and my wife when we called in to the café.) I said I wasn't interested in hearing Cloughie yap on. I'd kicked him up in the air many a time! But he kept on and on so eventually I agreed to go.

So off we went to the Dragon Hotel and we were sitting right over away from everybody which suited me. It was a total sell-out, with 600 people in attendance. Time was going by and Brian Clough hadn't arrived. Soon rumours were circulating that he wouldn't be there. He was winning everything at the time, including two European Cups, and was in such demand it was incredible. He was on the television all the time. I said, "Look, if Cloughie said he's going to be here, he'll be here. Don't worry about it."

Then, at about nine o'clock, in he walked, fresh from Nottingham and still in his tracksuit. They'd sent a Rolls-Royce up for him but they'd had a bit of trouble with traffic. He entered the room and in that famous accent of his, said, "Gentlemen, I'm very sorry I'm late, but I'm just going to go up to my room to get changed and I'll be back down in a few minutes." The whole room stood up and cheered. When he came back down, everybody stood again and applauded, then he joined the top table alongside the directors of Swansea City. On the other side of him were Tosh, Lawrie McMenemy and Max Boyce. On the table in front were the players who had won promotion for the Swans – Robbie, Curt, Jeremy Charles, Leighton James, the lot of them – all enjoying themselves and deservedly so. Lawrie got up and said a few words and Max sang a few songs. Then the directors got up to say a few words too, but the way they were talking suggested they attributed the success of the club to themselves, without mentioning the achievements of the players. I wasn't the only person to pick up on this.

Then Brian Clough got up and another cheer went around the room. There was silence as everybody waited to hear him speak. He began: "Well, I've never heard so much *bullshit* in all my life." He looked at the table with all the players on and said, "Boys, I don't know what you've been doing all season as it seems it's *these* people who have won promotion," – referring to the directors. The room erupted and people were falling about. So was I. I didn't check the reactions of the directors, though I imagine they were pretty gutted. It was so true what he said. If there was one thing Cloughie did, he always looked after his players. He wouldn't allow anyone to talk about them. In turn, they had to have their hair cut properly, dress immaculately and behave themselves. He was a typical England manager-in-waiting, but because he was so outspoken they denied him that position.

He talked for an hour before they eventually let him sit down. The night was coming to an end and everybody present wanted his autograph; they queued six abreast out through the doors. I was sitting with Peter Luprini and he was saying, "Mel, go and get his autograph for me!" I laughed off his request at first, but eventually gave in and went up to see him. I walked down behind the tables, saying hello and shaking hands with people as I knew most of them, until I was stood behind Cloughie with Peter's programme in my hand ready for signing. There was a commotion with people in the queue shouting for me to get his autograph for them, so Cloughie wondered what was going on and looked over his shoulder.

He saw me standing there and jumped up in the air with surprise. Next, he removed a director from the chair alongside him and said, "Sit down." He then went on, "How are you doing, young man?" I replied, "Oh, you know, struggling on," which was just a figure of speech I always used. He looked at me as if he was about to offer me a job, so I had to quickly come out with, "No, I'm alright, I'm doing nicely Bri …" He said, "Well, that's alright then, young man." We must have talked for about half an hour, but I'm convinced that if I hadn't stopped him he would have offered me a job, upon hearing me say I was struggling on. There was mutual respect there and it was nice. I've been to lots of dinners like this, but that night really stands out.

When I knew Cloughie back in my playing days he hardly drank, but I can imagine he went to dinners like this and sat on the top table all the time, constantly having drinks offered to him. It happened to me, although I didn't go to as many dinners as him, and it can get to the stage where you can offend people by refusing, so his drinking may have started there. As I mentioned earlier, Middlesbrough used the money they got for Brian Clough to buy me. It was a pity because it would have been nice to play in the same team.

The Toshack effect

I would never take anything away from what John Toshack did for Swansea City. The moment he was appointed manager *everything* changed: the club, the outlook of Swansea and the public's attitude. What he achieved was fantastic; the next five years were unbelievable. You have to remember just how low the club was when he was appointed. Not long before John arrived, and before I made my application to join the board, I was working on a house in Argyle Street. I'd taken the window out and was furiously shovelling concrete when three lads came down the road kicking a football. I was knackered but turned to these lads and said, "That's the way boys, you keep doing that and you'll be down the Vetch next year." One of the lads picked the ball up and shot back: "Who wants to go down the Vetch?" That was the mentality of the kids in Swansea. Well it hit me; I was sick.

All of a sudden, John was in charge and it was WOW! – the club was thriving. But if getting there is hard, staying there is another thing altogether. The club simply wasn't ready for that level of success and eventually it all started going wrong. It caught up with us. John was young at the time, only an inexperienced kid, though I'm not blaming him for it. That's football: ups and downs – and as quick as we went up we came back down. In effect we were back to where we started.

And then I became a director.

9

Save Our Swans

IDON'T KNOW WHAT HAPPENED in the boardroom, but Bobby Jones became chairman and invited me on to the board – for a fee. I was down in Penclawdd in Dove Lodge when he came to speak to me. I thought that maybe they had kept that letter from all those years before when I had previously applied to become a director.

Bobby came down in his Mercedes. My first reaction to his offer was to snatch his hand off, because I hadn't lost any of that desire to become a director. But I wouldn't give Bobby or the club the satisfaction. They'd ignored me in 1978 but now they were in trouble they came knocking. Eventually, of course, I took him up on his offer and they took three of us on: Harry Hyde, Dave Savage and myself.

Just visualise my first board meeting. After coming from a council house, rising up through the ranks of the playing staff, going on to Middlesbrough and Swindon then coming back, here I was, realising another ambition by joining the board. I didn't have a clue, however, what a board of directors actually *does*. I didn't know what the piece of paper in front of me with the minutes of the previous meeting was. I had a glance at it but didn't understand it.

Suddenly Bobby Jones announced he was standing

down as chairman of Swansea City as his car company had gone into liquidation and he could no longer hold the position. *Bloody hell*, we'd become directors under Bobby – it was he who had approached us – so the three of us hadn't expected that in the first meeting! All the directors were there: Doug Sharpe, Malcolm Struel, Peter Howard and Winston Rees. Most of them had held the position of chairman before. Myself, Dave Savage and Harry Hyde, said, "Don't look at us, we've only just joined." We were hoping to learn the ropes. So Winston was asked to become chairman and said he would, subject to Doug Sharpe becoming vice-chairman.

My first briefcase

I left the sheet of paper with the agenda and minutes on the table, not realising it was important, so during the next meeting I had no idea what they were referring to. You learnt as you went along. For example, with all the documentation that's flying around when you become a director, you need a briefcase to carry it. Coming from a council background, I would shove everything in a Tesco carrier bag. They'd shoot you for carrying a briefcase where I'm from! I feel a bit sensitive even now talking about it, but the truth is my wife bought one for me to stop me using the carrier bags – honest! That's how circumstances change you. I wasn't ready for it.

John Toshack was living up in Three Crosses in a lovely new estate with only about a dozen houses. One of our directors, Tom Phillips, was living there too, so I imagine they would have talked. Tom probably told him that if he was planning on coming back down the Vetch he'd better have a word with me. I had 17 acres of land down at Dove Lodge which I turned into a nine-hole golf course with a clubhouse. It was brilliant, and quite a challenging course. I was doing work on the swimming pool when a car pulled up. John got out and went in the boot of his car. I was laying concrete with Vic Gomersall who was living in a house there and going to run the country club complex. Vic looked up and saw it was Tosh, who greeted Vic as he went to get his golf clubs out. Vic walked across to see him, so I said, "Vic, where you going? Leave him alone, let's finish what we're doing." John put his clubs back in the boot and drove away. Tosh is a different person now; he's mellowed a bit. But his attitude was his strength and you respected him because of that. You still do.

At one of my first board meetings in 1985 the main topic for discussion was the team manager Colin Appleton. It was horrible. I was a novice in the boardroom, learning the ropes, and I felt for Colin. What happened to him wasn't fair. Swansea City were in no position to go out and buy players. The only new players we could recruit were trialists from places like Merthyr and Llanelli. They were no different to local league players in reality. For Colin to have to work with lads of that calibre in the Third Division of the Football League was diabolical.

I remember listening to them all in the boardroom discussing Colin's fate. I don't believe anybody ever wants to sack someone, but circumstances make you do things you don't want to do. I think it was the first time I had spoken up in a meeting. I said, "I tell you what: I'm very surprised at what's going on here today, because the position we've put Colin Appleton in ... well, I wouldn't fancy it. Have we ever *helped* him, have we ever given him any money to go and get anybody of any calibre?" Colin was waiting in the corridor outside the boardroom to be called in. He was expecting the worse and he had a black shirt and black suit on.

Colin came in, waiting to be sacked, but I'd talked the others round and we collectively decided to give him another chance. Winston Rees, who was chairman at this stage, said, "Colin, we don't think we've given you as much support as we should have and we want to be fair with you." He started crying and I felt really sorry for him. He was a good man but he didn't have a good time as Swansea manager. Shortly after this we had a game in the Welsh Cup; if I remember correctly it was at Newport. We lost, and Doug Sharpe, who was vice-chairman, took it upon himself to go in the dressing room at the end of the game and sack Colin on the spot. He didn't consult with the other directors. I knew *nothing* about that.

The name's Bond ...

Colin Appleton's successor was John Bond. Although I was a director, I didn't get involved in his appointment. I was happy just to be involved with the club, going to board meetings and watching all the games. It wasn't that I wasn't interested in the playing side of it, but I felt like I didn't want to interfere. Just because I was a past player, I didn't feel that meant I knew more than my fellow directors who hadn't played the game.

John Bond's role was that of public relations officer, in a sense. He had an assistant by the name of Fred Davies who was doing all the donkey work. John did it too, but he leaned more towards the press; if they came down he would always be there, while Fred would take the heavy duty training. It was actually a good balance and they complemented each other.

We played against Bristol City down the Vetch. We were all in the boardroom, along with the visiting directors, when all of a sudden John Bond came in. He was always immaculately dressed with suit and tie, hair always smart, and he was a big man so he had a presence. Terry Cooper, the ex-Leeds defender who was manager of Bristol City, told his chairman that their coach was ready. So we said our goodbyes and John closed the door behind them. "Right," he said, "I want to speak to all you gentlemen now and find out what you know about football." I was laughing inside though I wasn't showing it in my face. I'd played against him when I was a kid and he was at West Ham. But then I started thinking, "What a nerve he's got! We employ him as a manager and here he is dictating to us." I had only just joined the board so I was inexperienced, but after another season or so he would never have got away with it. We ran the club and paid his wages. But I just sat in the corner and thought, this is going to be interesting.

He started off with one of the directors: "Who have *you* played for?" "Er … I played at Ammanford," came the reply. "*Ammanford?*" he said. "*Where the **** is that?*" He went through all the directors with names like Haverfordwest being mentioned. They'd all played but hadn't had the gift to turn professional – though of course they'd all gone on to become professional people in their own areas. John went right around the room; it was unbelievable. He was taking the mickey out of the people who were employing him. He bypassed me and went straight to whoever was sitting to my right. I would have loved him to have approached me! Though saying that, I think I would have got upset and said something.

I think the reason John took this tone with the directors was because their box was right behind the dugout, so he would hear a lot of what was being said. The directors were, and are, basically supporters, and just like supporters they give vent to their feelings. (Are they not supposed to?) However, as a past player I could relate to the players in a different way to people who hadn't been in that situation, so I would hold back on the outbursts. This particular incident blew over, but there was a lot more turmoil just around the corner.

Baptism of fire

The club owed £86,000 to the VAT man. It was a body blow and I wondered how it had been allowed to go on so long without being paid. But when you've got seven or eight people on a board, you can't have them all getting involved in the day-to-day running. Somehow, between us, we had to find that sum quickly. I was putting in £10,000. I didn't want to as I'd only recently put money in to become a director, but I knew I had to. Others put in what they could afford – £6,000 or whatever. Once we had all put in we realised we were still short by £10,000. Doug Sharpe said, "Look, you're wasting your time, lads. Forget about the VAT. I'll pay it, but I want control of the club." I didn't mind because I didn't have designs on owning the club, I was happy just to be a part of it. Nevertheless, we were all shocked that Doug had offered to pay the full amount. I wondered if he was in a position to do so, as he had his own business to run. The VAT man would probably have accepted a shortfall, but Doug assured us that he would take care of it. We left that meeting believing the matter was in hand.

A few months later the club arranged a tour to the Far East, to Kuala Lumpur. Doug Sharpe had organised it and he was going over there with the squad as chairman because Winston Rees had things to do in Swansea. At a board meeting before this trip, Doug picked up a big pile of documents and placed it in front of me. His very words to me were: "Mel, we need a ground safety certificate – do your best," and he was off. I hadn't seen any documentation relating to this situation and it was my first involvement in the serious administration of the club. I didn't know what to do, but I took this pile of papers home and went through them slowly and carefully. I realised I had to deal with a range of important people to pull this off: the chief of police, the chief fire officer, someone from County Hall and another gentleman from the Guildhall. I had to arrange a meeting and bring everyone together. It was the start of a week that can only be described as a baptism of fire for me as a new director.

The day of the meeting I made sure we had new tablecloths on the tables and that we had coffee and pastries. Everything had to be correct. We all sat down and the chief of police in all his gear – the full uniform and finery – leaned forward and said, "Excuse me, Mel, if you don't mind me asking, where's the gentleman by the name of Mr Sharpe?" I said, "I'm sorry sir, but the club has gone on a tour overseas and he's with them out there." He couldn't believe it. He said, "Are you telling me that the meetings we've had previously are forgotten about? Are we starting afresh again?"

I didn't know there had been any previous meetings

or any dialogue on the matter as I'd been so poorly informed. I was looking at him and I was lost for words. I put my hands together and said, "God help me!" The gentleman from County Hall could see I was in a very awkward situation and said, "Look, we're here now – let's see what we can do." From that moment on, everyone began working toward the common goal of attaining a Ground Safety Act certificate and they helped me tremendously. I had to learn fast as I didn't use to say much in board meetings; we had people like Tom Phillips and Malcolm Struel who had been there years so I felt like I was junior to them. The fact that I'd played football was immaterial.

There was a hell of a lot to be done at the Vetch. The Bradford City fire disaster had just happened and many had tragically lost their lives. Fire officers had to address football clubs because stadiums hadn't been looked upon as dangerous places prior to the disaster, certainly not in the way they were afterwards. Two of our stands – the West Stand and the Centre Stand – were made of timber, so the fire officer wanted everything cleared from underneath them. Over the years, bits of paper and drink cartons had fallen down the gaps. It was a nightmare but it had to be cleared because if a lit cigarette dropped down there, the stand would have gone up in flames. All the same, it was a *horrible* job.

The North Bank wasn't too bad, though the crush barriers had to be rearranged. We had to put fences up and get surveyors in, along with structural engineers. All the guttering had to be changed. Then we had to have new access routes in the stands and cut rights of way out. If there were thirty seats in a row we had to restrict it to twenty or so by taking seats out. While I was taking seats away, season-ticket holders would come to the ground knowing I was doing alterations and say, "Don't take that seat, Mel, I've been sitting there for thirty years!" The irony was that we were getting very poor crowds at the time!

While everyone else was in Kuala Lumpur, we didn't stop for a week. Everyone pulled together and it progressed really well. I had myself and three lads working non-stop and I was paying their wages.

I was sitting on the pitch taking a break when the secretary, Pat Abramson, came up and asked if I could take a look at some player contracts. They had run out and we needed to renew them before sending them off to Lytham St Anne's for registration. I said, "Pat, leave it for the moment – leave it until the chairman is here and he can address it." I didn't want to get involved as I had enough on my plate with the fire certificate.

Hold the fort

Days went by and Pat would say, "Mel, we're running out of time here. The players won't be registered before the start of the season if we don't deal with it now." Eventually I went into the office and had a look. She showed me a handful of contracts which I looked at closely. There were figures on two of the contracts that I couldn't understand. As a board of directors, we had agreed that no player would earn more than £250 a week without express permission from the board. However, there were amounts of money on these contracts which I knew we hadn't agreed to, £100 above say, so I wouldn't sign them. I was clearly naïve to a lot of things that were going on down there. "Hang on a minute," I said to Pat, "where are the other contracts kept?" They were in John Bond's office. I went in there as I was entitled to, being a director, and pulled out the folder of contracts. There were at least five players on higher wages than we had agreed. Well, this can't be! I thought. I wasn't happy about it. I photocopied the five dubious contracts blank, signed them and gave them to Pat to send off, and kept the originals in my briefcase.

The business with the contracts was troubling me, but this was just the start. The next day I was out on the pitch with a few lads, working out what to do to the ground next, when Pat told me, "Mel, there's a gentleman from the electricity board here." I said, "And?" "Well, he wants to get paid," she said. "Well pay him, then," I replied. "We haven't got any money in the office," she said. We looked in all the offices at the ground but there was nothing. I went to see the man and asked if he could come back a bit later in the afternoon. He said, "I'm sorry but I'm not leaving here until I get paid. I've been here twice before and I've been told to come back later on both occasions." His boss had told him to come down and issue us with an ultimatum: pay the bill or the electricity will be cut off. "I'm not leaving here until I've done one or the other," he pledged. "Will you take a cheque off me, then?" I suggested. "I don't care who it comes from," he said, "as long as I've got something to hand in." I took him out to my van and wrote out a cheque for £475, thinking I'd be reimbursed by the club. The minute he had the cheque in his hand, he said, "Since when have you been paying the bills? You must be off your head!" I looked at him stunned, as he seemed to know more about what the club was going through than I did. And I never did get reimbursed.

Crisis of conscience

Another matter upon which I was totally in the dark was that the club were in a tribunal with the council regarding the redevelopment of the Vetch Field. These plans had been put into place before I joined the board. The club wanted to expand and build on the ground, but for this they would have to acquire many of the surrounding properties in Glamorgan Street, William Street and Madoc Street. The people living in these houses strongly objected to the plans, as I would have myself. Apart from anything else, I had a crisis of conscience because I knew all the residents personally. I'd lived streets away from them in the Sandfields area for years, so I didn't want to be opposing them. I was torn.

I had to attend a tribunal on the Thursday on behalf of the club; I couldn't just bury my head in the sand. I phoned our solicitor but he told me he wasn't going to represent us because he was owed £10,000 by the club and until this outstanding debt was settled he wouldn't be in our corner. It seemed like Swansea City was collapsing like a house of cards. I went up to his offices in Walter Road but he was adamant. When I got home I asked my wife, "How the hell am I going to get around this?" I went back to the club solicitor, asked him to put aside his grievances with the club and told him that I would pay for the two days in the tribunal. He accepted that, attended the hearing, then sent me a bill for £5,000. I couldn't believe it. How that figure was justified for two days' work I'll never know. I refused to pay it and took *him* to court. Nobody in Swansea would represent me because they all know each other, so I had to go to someone in Cardiff.

I found myself standing in the dock. It was an environment I was totally unfamiliar with and I wanted to keep it that way as it's not a nice situation. I had an inch-thick dossier in front of me and questions coming from all angles, being asked to go to page 105 and what have you. The judge asked me, "Are you *sure* you're a director of Swansea City, because you don't seem to know much about these matters." I tried to explain that all this related to before my time. The situation with the residents and the tribunal was taken out of my hands when the chairman returned, but along the way I had to pay £5,000 and other costs as well. You couldn't make it up really.

While all this chaos was going on, none of the other directors came to the ground. Just imagine if the electricity man had gone away and switched off the electric: Swansea City Football Club finished for £475! Though I was realising that sum was just the tip of a very large iceberg.

Every morning I would come into town and get down to the Vetch for about nine o'clock. This particular morning I didn't realise the touring party had returned from Kuala Lumpur. I was also met by the officials concerned with the fire safety certificate, standing in the tunnel leading onto the pitch. It took me by surprise to see them all there. I had done everything they had asked of me to the best of my ability. In fairness, the police and fire people wanted the best for the club. They didn't want to close it down but they were obliged to be rigorous in their approach. "Good morning gentlemen, what's wrong?" I asked. They said, "Well, we've been summoned down here by Mr Sharpe." I couldn't believe it. I went and sat in with Pat and listened to it unfold.

Doug really put his foot in it. He had called the officials in for nine o'clock (they arrived dead-on) and then turned up late himself. At 9.30 he still wasn't there. Then in he came, like the Lord Mayor of Swansea. He said, "Gentlemen, I think you're being *really harsh* on the club." He basically accused them of trying to block the club in its efforts to attain the safety certificate; he hadn't bothered to check what had been going on in his absence. The chief fire officer put him on the spot and practically frog-marched him down the tunnel to show him the work we'd done.

Time for action

I still had to get to the bottom of the contracts business, so at the next board meeting I spoke up. I said, "I'd like to bring up a situation with regards to the wage structure at the club. The chairman and the vice-chairman have been agreeing to wages that are way above what we agreed." I was paying out left, right and centre – as were other directors – so I was not there for personal gain. There was no way I was going to allow anyone to go above me and get away with it. Bobby Jones said, "Hold on, Mel, let's carry on with the meeting ..." I said, "Bob, I'm telling you that there are contracts being signed that exceed the sums that we've all agreed on." They didn't want to believe me. At this point I started to panic a bit, thinking I may have misread them and made an embarrassing mistake. But I had a quick glance at them and realised I was right. I put one of the contracts on the table. "There we are: have a look at that," I said. "Mel, let's just carry on with the meeting," they said. I was adamant: "No, no, let's discuss *this* first." They didn't want to look really, but just to shut me up, Bobby Jones leaned over and looked at it. "Christ!" he said. "Mel is right!" The other directors wished to see it now and tried to get the contract off Bobby. I said, "Gentlemen, don't worry about that – *have one each*," and I placed the other four contracts on the table. Talk about putting a cat among the pigeons.

Winston Rees, the chairman, put his briefcase on the table and put his documents back in it. He closed the briefcase, stood up and said, "I resign." He walked out. Doug Sharpe did the same. I was gobsmacked. Where was the openness and discussion that you should have in any boardroom? They walked out leaving the five of us there – Harry Hyde, Dave Savage, Bobby Jones, Peter Howard and myself.

Black Friday

The next day I was at home in Penclawdd, working out in the fields in my tractor. My wife called me to say Pat Abramson was on the telephone. Pat said, "Mel, you'd better get in straight away." I said, "What do you mean? What's going on?" She replied, "They've closed the gates. They've closed the club." I started laughing. "What do you mean they've closed the club?" She said, "Well, they've put chains on the gates, they're saying we've gone bankrupt." I knew she was serious because she was crying, so I said, "Pat, I'll be in in a minute." I rushed straight to the Vetch as I was, in my working gear.

I got down there and sure enough the gates were locked. I managed to get in and discovered the VAT man had been in and closed us down. It transpired that

Swansea City Football Club still owed £86,000. None of the directors knew that the matter we'd discussed some months earlier hadn't been addressed. Doug Sharpe had assured us he would deal with it.

John Bond was going around the dressing room kicking the doors in. That proved it was a total surprise to him. He was fuming because the board of directors had failed him. The administrator was Jeffrey Payne in St Helen's Road. He did everything he could to help us but ultimately he had a job to do. Even though Pat had phoned everyone, the only other director who came down to the Vetch on that terrible day was Peter Howard. It was left to me to go into the dressing room and tell the players that as of now, they were free agents. The only thing they could take from the ground was a pair of boots. "Put your clothes back on," I said, as they were ready to go training. I remember Jimmy Rimmer and Tommy Hutchison, the two senior players, were there. They all sat very quietly, in shock, wondering where they were going to go and what they were going to do. This all happened overnight. These boys didn't see it coming, neither did the directors. But the chairman and vice-chairman knew. They *must* have known.

The Big Five

I was totally gutted. For the next three days I practically lived down the Bryn, a very exclusive place between Swansea and Mumbles, with Peter Howard. Peter, Harry, Dave, Bobby and myself – or the 'Big Five' as we became known in the press – would go there first thing in the morning and come away very late at night, trying to work out what we could do. I must pay a compliment to Betty Howard for putting up with us over those couple of days and for keeping us going with coffee and sandwiches. She was wonderful.

All of the people on the board had their own businesses, but nobody had ever gone into administration, liquidation or company voluntary arrangements. We'd never sampled that sort of crisis so we were at a disadvantage. I didn't even understand what it *meant*, to be honest.

We knew we had to get the money to pay the VAT man, so first we employed Bob Nettleship as our solicitor and Nigel Davies as our barrister. Nigel's chambers were in London and he helped us put in an application to see if we could about-turn the decision to close Swansea City and keep the club alive. We were to have our case heard at the High Court in London at ten o'clock this particular morning. I'd turned my home in Penclawdd into a country club and we were busy, staying up until two o'clock, and I had to get the six o'clock train out of Swansea High Street. It was pointless me going to bed. We dared not miss that train because if we didn't get to London on time the club would be gone. To make sure, I was at the station with a couple of hours to spare. The only place that was open was the café over the road. I went over for a coffee and the lady standing behind the counter said, "Hello – don't you recognise me?" I said, "No – should I?" She said, "Can you remember coming down Carmarthen Road ..." I said, "No, don't tell me ..."

The night before the Swans played Manchester United in the friendly I mentioned earlier, I was driving to Gendros, taking my girlfriend (now my wife) back to her home. It was about half-eight and I wanted to be tucked up by nine o'clock ahead of the big game the following day. As I was coming down Carmarthen Road a young lady walked out right in front of me. BANG! I hit her down the road. My girlfriend started to panic; she couldn't speak. A long queue of people at a bus stop ran across to see if she was okay. I pushed through the crowd and said, "Are you alright, love?" She said something to me, then I picked her up and put her in the car and took her down to Singleton Hospital. I made sure she was safe there and went up to the police station. They kept me in until two in the morning. I was trying to get an early night!

This was the same young lady standing behind the counter some 25 years later. All I could think to say was, "Are you alright?" She said, "Yes, I'm fine." They had kept her in hospital for three days. I hadn't known the outcome in all that time. Anyway, after she served me my coffee, Peter Howard arrived and we got on our train to London. Although there were five of us who had put this bid together, it was only felt necessary for the two of us to go. We'd had to get £20,000 together as a bond to get a stay of execution for the club. It was quite a bit of money in those days, but between the five of us we raised it.

Court short

We were met by Bob Nettleship and the three of us went on to Nigel Davies' chambers. We had a quick talk and then walked from there to the High Court. We walked through all these corridors past other people going bankrupt as well, until we reached our chamber. It was like a maze. We sat outside waiting to be called, when suddenly a group of about fifteen people appeared at the end of the corridor. It was Doug Sharpe, with a load of associates and business people. We stood up to greet them and say, "Well done lads, thanks for the moral support," sort-of-thing. But they walked straight past and ignored us. This was very strange as it was *our* application that had gone in. Bob Nettleship and Nigel Davies were totally taken aback by this because they didn't know what was going on internally at the club.

It was a big courtroom with Judge Scott presiding over our application. We were sat there, the four of us, and Doug Sharpe's party were across the way. We just listened while Nigel Davies did the talking, as he was the barrister. Every time Nigel would say something, the other group's solicitor would get up and make a grander proclamation. We were both there for the same end, but it was our appeal that was being heard. We didn't know why they chose to ignore us or why they were trying to usurp us in court. They came unstuck though, because Judge Scott kept saying, "Sit down." They kept interfering and it made for crossed purposes. Eventually they granted us a ten-day extension to come up with the money to pay the VAT and rescue the club. Gordon Taylor from the PFA was there and he did a lot of work to help things along.

In effect we had two weeks to come up with the £86,000 and a survival package to take the club forward. We came out of the High Court and were very excited. Doug Sharpe's party had disappeared. We got back to Paddington station and the *Evening Standard* ran a story saying: 'Nurse – A stitch in time saves club.' They had a photo of me throwing my hat in the air in jubilation outside the court.

Doug Sharpe and his party were very clever; they had gone up by road and were back in Swansea before we had even left Paddington. Meanwhile, Peter Howard and myself had got on a train to come home and were told that we'd have to pay an extra £40 if we wanted to get on that particular train, so we waited for the next one. It was okay; we had a cup of tea and a bun to celebrate while we waited.

We had a friendly fund-raising game with Manchester United arranged that night and Doug's party got back nice and early to take all the adulation. They went out on the pitch celebrating, saying, "We've rescued Swansea City!" We got back halfway through the game and everyone was looking at us like we were nothing. But they hadn't rescued the club, the 'Big Five' had. This has never been widely understood, but there are people who can verify it. Doug Sharpe just got back to Swansea quicker than us! It's farcical really.

As far as we were concerned, when we went to the High Court our objective was simply to save the club, or get a stay-of-execution. We made our application without any thought of who would run the club should we be successful. Though it was our application that was accepted, Doug Sharpe assumed control of the club. No-one challenged this as we didn't have designs on running the club anyway. Ultimately we didn't care who took over. All we were concerned about was the job in hand – rescuing Swansea City.

Save Our Swans

The club still had to raise money. We had been all over town collecting in places like Swansea Market and the public had been brilliant. Everyone was sponsoring the five people who were trying to save the club. Doug Sharpe arranged a meeting at the Patti Pavilion to ask shareholders to surrender their bonds and to accept a penny in the pound for them, as this was in effect a debt the club had. Then the money the 'Big Five' had helped raise was signed over to Doug and he was able to pay off the debt.

I know I've given Doug a bit of a slating, but this is the truth as I know it. However, from the moment he took charge, Swansea City Football Club prospered for the next thirteen years and everything was rosy at the Vetch Field. He deserves a lot of credit for bringing people like Terry Yorath and Frank Burrows to the club. He ran a tight ship by himself and you never heard of the club struggling financially again during his tenure as chairman.

After Doug's takeover I reverted to being a supporter, as did the other directors. I had always renewed my two season tickets for the Centre Stand during my time on the board. Everything that had gone before was history. Peter Howard was the only one who walked away; he had put a bit more money in than the rest of us and felt he had been burnt. To this day I still see Dave Savage and Bobby Jones at the Liberty Stadium. Harry Hyde isn't too well at the moment, or otherwise he'd be there too.

As a director of Swansea City you don't get paid; it costs *you* money. Every time you go down there you're laying out money – it's unbelievable. When eight of you are sitting around a table and you have to find £10,000 by the weekend and there's no money in the bank, that's the harsh reality of it. I've seen it. The public outside don't realise what's going on. I would imagine every supporter thinks if you're a director you take money out. That is furthest from the truth. The two times I've been involved in the boardroom it has cost me heavily ...

10

Why Me?

I LIKED TONY PETTY AS a *person*. I respected him, though what he did was wrong in my eyes. I'm a local and I love the club; I want to see it go on and progress, whereas he was looking at it as an investment. We had two different objectives, but he was very intelligent and I liked him.

Before Tony Petty purchased Swansea City in 2001 I had been a director for about a year, maybe two. Doug Sharpe had sold the club to a company called Silver Shield in 1997, which consisted of David Farmer, Neil McClure, Alan Wicks, Martin Burgess and Steve Hamer. Steve knew that I had been a director previously and had helped the club to survive back in 1985, so they approached me and asked if I'd like to become a director again. Well, of course I did; football and the Swans is all I've lived for. The first thing I did was ask if they required any money from me, because my previous experience of that position was of paying out all the time – or so it seemed.

To my relief they said no, they didn't require any money from me as they were financially sound. They'd just like my input. They told me they were going forward and were hoping to develop the Morfa Stadium as a new home as the council were talking about taking the Vetch back for development. Towards the end of Doug's time as chairman, he had negotiated with the council and acquired a new fifty-year lease on the Vetch. This was a major coup for the club and I doubt whether many other people could have got the Vetch back on a £400-a-week rental, so I give Doug credit for that. I'd been on the board for about twelve months when Silver Shield changed their name to Ninth Floor, as they were diversifying into different things.

Déjà vu

Just like when I'd joined the board in the 1980s, one of my first meetings as a director was to discuss sacking the team manager, who at this time was John Hollins. I felt terrible because I don't like to let anybody go. John was a great lad and had done a lot of good things for the club, including winning the Third Division Championship in the 1999/2000 season, but the other directors had decided we needed a change. John came in and Mike Lewis told him we wouldn't be renewing his contract and were asking him to resign. He didn't like it at all.

Not long before John's departure we took on a player called Mamady Sidibe who was from France, though of African origin. He stayed at my hotel when he arrived in Swansea, along with his brother. They were both massive fellas. John Hollins dropped 'Big Mama' (as he became known) outside my hotel on his first day at the club and told him to come and see me, knowing I was a director. Sidibe couldn't speak a word of English at that time. I was sitting outside with Mel Charles, who asked him if he'd had anything to eat. He just looked back blankly. "Food?" said Mel again, gesturing to eat. Sidibe made a gesture to his pockets to suggest he didn't have any money. I said, "What do you mean you've got no money? And you've had no food?" Which was pointless because he couldn't understand. I reached in my pocket and gave him a £20 note. He took it off me and quick as a flash he was gone!

Now, surely the club should have made sure that he was looked after, food-wise at the very least. They must have thought that I was responsible for looking after him because he was staying at my hotel. I wasn't charging the club for his stay and he wasn't there long before they sorted him out a flat over the marina. I didn't mind because I was a director, but it gives you an idea of how the club was being run. He wasn't with the Swans for long before he moved to Stoke City.

A couple of months earlier, John Hollins had come to the board and asked if he could bring Alan Curtis in as his assistant. The club jumped at that because Alan was already at the club doing a good job with the kids. I approached him and said, "Al, do you realise what you're doing? The position you are holding at the moment means you will be at the club for life." I explained that if he took on the assistant role and John went, he would be likely to go with him. Alan wanted to do it though, so he relinquished his duties with the kids and joined John's management team. When it came time to release John Hollins, inevitably we had to release Alan as well. Nobody wanted to because he's a nice fella, as everybody knows. Curt's a legend in Swansea, always will be, because of his standing in the city and at the club. We brought Al in and told him that we were bringing somebody new to the club and that they would want to have their own guy, so he had to go. He accepted that and just walked away.

Colin Addison's name came up for consideration, so Mike Lewis and I went to see him in the Vale of Glamorgan. This was the first time I'd been directly involved in appointing a new manager. Colin was concerned he wouldn't be able to have his assistant, Peter Nicholas, with him, but we told him the two vacancies existed so they joined the club. Colin did a fine job but the club got into difficulties and Ninth Floor wanted to sell it on. Mike Lewis was charged with finding a buyer.

Roger and out

We played QPR in the FA Cup at the Vetch and beat them 4-0. Roger Freestone played a blinder in goal for us. A few months after this game, QPR lost their first-choice goalkeeper through injury and, remembering how well Roger had performed in the Cup match against them, they came in for him. They offered Roger a three-year contract, £50,000 in his hand and treble his wages. But he had only just bought a new house in Newport and had a sense of loyalty to Swansea City, so he turned it down. He respected the club and the supporters who he felt had been fantastic to him.

I was in the office when he turned it down. I said, "Rog, let me first say, on behalf of the club and the public of Swansea, thank you. I respect you for that. But personally, I think you must be ****ing brain-dead!" I didn't want him to go, but being a past player myself and realising how the system works, I had to give him this advice. I turned out to be right, because not long after this the club sacked him. For all his loyalty, they just turned their backs on him and threw him out. It was shoddy treatment of a wonderful servant who had given us fantastic service over ten or so years. In his last game they should have taken him off early so he could accept the acclaim of the crowd, but they didn't. It was 'here today, gone tomorrow' – and that wasn't right.

Troubled times. Again

Ninth Floor Plc had been trying to get the go-ahead for the new stadium for about five years, but nothing was coming of it and they were losing a lot of money – close to a million pounds annually. Initially they were quite prepared to do that, figuring that the end-product would bail them out. They believed they were going to have the franchise to develop the new stadium but the council were always intending to do it themselves. All of a sudden Ninth Floor realised it wasn't going to happen, so they wanted to sell the club. They offered it for £1m: the club shop on Willliam Street and the car park was worth £200,000 and they wanted £800,000 for the shares. The ground was leased from the council, so they owned the club but not the ground. I've got nothing but praise for those guys because they had helped the club survive for a few years before this.

Another gentleman people criticise is Mike Lewis, who was general manager at this time. Now, I like Mike, he's a nice fella and I got on great with him. If he was to drive past here now I'd invite him in for a drink. They made Mike chairman and David Farmer and I were directors, along with Don Goss – another one who did well for the club. The club was changing and these guys helped change it; they created Cyril the Swan, for example.

I'd go down the club most mornings and ask Mike Lewis if there was any progress with the sale. There were some interested parties, including an ex-player living in America whose name escapes me, but time was going by and nothing was really forthcoming. I decided, with the blessing of Mike and the other directors, to build a bar on the North Bank because there was no other money coming in apart from the Harry Griffiths Bar behind the Centre Stand. I was trying to generate some revenue outside of season tickets and gate money. I paid for new toilets and helped out as best I could. They didn't ask me for any money but I was quite happy to do whatever I could if it was beneficial for the club.

Back to work on the North Bank

Don Goss had just acquired a licence to serve alcohol on the North Bank. I knew that part of the ground well as it hadn't changed in all the years I had been there. I couldn't envisage where we could sell alcohol from, so one day Don, Mike Lewis and I went around to have a look. They showed me a shed that was six feet wide and three feet deep. At this time I owned the Seahaven, the Tudor Court and the St Helen's on Oystermouth Road – all licensed premises – so I knew the problems and requirements of serving alcohol. I couldn't believe we would be allowed to serve from this little hut. My first thought was: how are five or six thousand people on the North Bank going to get a drink at half-time from here?

So the first thing I did was go down and see Billy the Forge, a steel and metal guy in Swansea. He came up and we put a covering over a section from the back of the North Bank which was about thirty feet long and seven feet wide. He put all the girders up and I fitted all the timber, so at least we could protect a couple of hundred fans from the elements. It was good, but I wasn't happy with it. I noticed there could be some space behind the boards under the terrace, so the next day we had JCBs gutting it out. I did it in line with what the fire officers, council planners and police wanted and they were all satisfied with it. Most days I'd be working on this bar and my friend Robert Ridgeway, who is a fanatical supporter of the Swans, would come by to see how I was progressing. We'd go for a rest on the terrace and look out on the pitch and imagine what we could do with the place if we won the lottery.

It took two or three months during the close season to build the bar and it opened at the first game. I was asked to do the opening, and the minute I did I handed the keys to Mike Lewis and said, "There you are – it's yours." It had cost almost £40,000 out of my own pocket but it was my choice and I wanted to do it for the club. Straight away it was generating a couple of thousand pounds every game and was so busy you couldn't get in the place. It was maintenance-free because the floor was slabbed and it worked a treat. For years, though, the Vetch Field wasn't utilised to its full potential, and if you look at the Liberty Stadium and all the various facilities for generating income today, it really is a different world.

The sale of the club was really troubling me, just as it was Mike Lewis, as no-one was coming forward. As well as this concern, I remember thinking to myself, "What if somebody from outside buys the club, or somebody buys the club car park or the club shop – what's the club going to do if they don't allow us to use them?" So I bought both the shop and car park as freehold properties to safeguard them. I allowed the club to use both without charge. I was just happy that they were protected.

Alongside this, my fear was that if the club couldn't find a buyer and went into receivership or liquidation, the main body controlling it would also be the biggest creditor. At the time it was Ninth Floor, with the £800,000 worth of shares. So I invited Alan Wicks, the chairman of Ninth Floor, to offer the share capital to a panel of local business people who I thought wanted to play a part in the club's survival.

Unfortunately, for all their good intentions, they couldn't accept what Alan was asking. They said, "We don't want to go down that road, but if Mel wants to he can." They threw the ball right back at me. I didn't know *what* to feel, but I thought, "Bloody hell, I can't handle that!" I had wanted to help but I hadn't bargained for this. I told my wife, "I'm going to have to do something here – I'm going to have to buy the club my-bloody-self." I had press and reporters at my hotel every day; I was afraid to come in the place.

Alan Wicks had given Mike Lewis three months to find a prospective buyer. Time was running out and there was nobody coming forward. We had a charity football match in Clyne to raise money for the club and I remember thinking to myself, "They're leaving it late now." I couldn't put myself out on a limb – I'm not that wealthy. So I offered Mike the sum of £400,000 for the shares, using my own collateral, but then I found out that would only buy me a third of them. That was no good to me because they'd be taking my money and still telling me what to do. I couldn't accept that. The next thing I knew, Mike had sold it to a London-based businessman called Tony Petty for £1.

Enter Tony Petty

Tony Petty could have relieved me of my position as director instantly. He really slipped up by not releasing me because if he had, I wouldn't have been able to do anything against him. One reason he may have kept me on was that no cheques could go out from the club unless I'd counter-signed them, as I'd had a long relationship with Lloyds, the club's bankers. Tony quickly realised the club was in trouble financially, as everyone did, and he didn't have millions to put in. He wasn't a Swansea person so he had no allegiance to the club or the city; it was purely a business transaction to him so he cut his cloth accordingly.

The way he did it was to say that anybody earning over £250 a week had to go. They couldn't be retained and were to be offered freedom of contract. This would leave us as a football club with just kids. It wouldn't be fair to them, it wouldn't be fair to the public and it wouldn't be fair to the club. Also, if other were clubs looking at our players, Tony wanted to sell them straight away. He wasn't knowledgeable on football. He let our biggest asset, young Stuart Roberts, go to Wycombe Wanderers for just £100,000 when he was worth much more. Every day he would go over to the club shop and take the money in the name of balancing the books. He was stripping everything. Now, I'm a Swansea person, a past player and I love the club so I couldn't let that happen.

I thought, "Enough's enough and this has got to be sorted out," because we were going to go out of the league and out of business. A year after Petty we nearly went into the Conference, but many of the playing staff were still there. That was the legacy of the Petty days. That said, I don't resent him at all. If you are offered something on a plate, like real money and a genuine profit, you're going to take it. He didn't realise what he was doing and I truly believe he thought he was doing the correct thing. The problem was he wanted to run a football club like a normal business, which you can't do. This business is in the public domain. His philosophy of 'if you can't afford to pay somebody they've got to go' is a basic rule of business, but applying it to football was wrong. I'd heard he'd been involved with a club in Australia and it had all gone wrong, but as far as I was concerned that was hearsay, so I took him as I found him. What he'd done before and what he did after was none of my business; I wasn't interested and it wasn't for me to judge.

Another misconception is that Tony was never in Swansea. He was here five days out of seven. Every day Mike Lewis, Tony Petty and his associate John Shuttleworth would come to my hotel and we'd have a couple of drinks before walking a few doors up to the Abertawe for something to eat. Tony would try desperately to change my attitude towards him and see his way of thinking. I'd sit on one side and they'd sit on the other and they'd say, "Mel, don't *fight* us, we have to do this and we have to do that," etc etc. To which I said, "No, what you are doing is leaving the club destitute, and the road you are taking us down will take us out of existence."

I never fell out with Petty, never argued with him, I just said, "Tone, you're doing the wrong thing – you can't do that." I've often asked myself why it was left down to me. The lads who are doing a fantastic job in 2009 were involved at the time but none of them wanted to do it. I'd like to acknowledge and pay a big compliment to Steve Hamer for inviting me to re-join the board those few years earlier, and in doing so putting me in the position to help the club further down the line.

Charlo

Mel Charles doesn't have to say anything to make you laugh, you just have to look at him. He's a comic in his own right. He's a real character and we go everywhere together.

In early 2002 we went to a football dinner just outside Cardiff, an annual affair organised by a big company called Just Rentals. He had rung me early that morning to ask what time I planned to leave. I asked him why and he explained we'd be having a few drinks so he'd arranged for somebody to drive him up and back. He then rang back a little later to say this guy had let him down and could he travel with me. He thought I would use my car, the Rolls-Royce I'd had for twenty years. He was looking forward to arriving in the Rolls. I'd told him to come around for midday as the function was at four and I wanted to leave in good time. I came down from my apartment into the hotel lounge and Mel was sitting under the stairs looking terrified. He'd arrived looking for me and a new member of my staff, not knowing who he was, had let him in and told him to wait under the stairs! Mel hadn't expected that because he's used to people knowing him, especially around Swansea.

Anyway, I told him to get in the van. "The *what*?" he said. "The van. We're going up in the van," I replied. "Oh, I thought we were going up in the car." We drove up with Mel in the passenger seat and myself sitting on the handbrake because I had someone driving. When we eventually got there it took Charlo half and hour to get out because his legs had stiffened up. (His son Jeremy was a great player but he had the same problem with his knees and that's what stopped his career early.)

Charlo was struggling but eventually we got through the French doors and in. It was a beautiful venue, with a big staircase leading up to a banqueting hall. It was very plush, lovely carpets and furnishings, but it was all blue! Charlo pulled himself up the rail and I ran past him. "What do you think you're doing," he shouted after me, "are you making a comeback?" We took our seats and I gave Malcolm, the driver, £20 and told him to get the drinks in. He came back with two each for the three of us – I think Charlo had caught us up by this stage – and gave me back the £20. "What's this all about?" I asked. "The drinks are on the house," he replied. Charlo jumped up and said, "I'll get the next round!" We had a good laugh about that!

There were six hundred or so at the dinner, including the likes of Jackie Charlton, but the majority were Cardiff people. I'd had my battles on the pitch with Brian Clark and Tosh but I respected Cardiff, always have done. They were honouring Alan Curtis that evening, among others, and he got up to say a few words. As he was about to finish he turned everyone's attention to the problems at Swansea City and said, "There's a gentleman in the room who is doing his best to save the club: Mr Mel Nurse."

Well, I wasn't expecting anything like that. I was trying to get under the table to hide because I felt embarrassed. I've always liked to do things quietly, without any fuss. The whole room got up and everyone was clapping and clambering to our table to offer support. These were Cardiff people as well. I've got to be honest: I very rarely cry but there were tears in my eyes that night.

Taking back the Swans

There was a public outcry when Tony Petty tried to attend a match. He attempted to get to the boardroom but was met with too much opposition, so he went up to the East Stand and into a lounge away from the general public. Soon after this, and not on a match day, Tony was in his office in the East Stand and a load of supporters had congregated outside the ground. They were going to shoot him, burn down the ground; it was getting ridiculous. I was sitting in my hotel at the time, quietly thinking to myself, and realising only Tony and I could sort this out. It had reached a point where he wouldn't deal with anybody else because the bad feeling was so intense.

I phoned him and asked where he was. "I'm in the Vetch, Mel," he said. "Jesus, they're all outside ... I daren't leave these offices." He was terrified. I arranged to go down there, but in the back way. One of the ground staff snuck me in. Tony realised he couldn't go any further and wanted to sell his shares back to me. It was time for him to leave. I asked him what he wanted. He mentioned a figure and I shook hands with him quickly. I don't know how he got out of there that day but I was just happy that we'd done the deal.

We arranged to conduct the transaction in Cardiff; it couldn't be done in Swansea because of the mood of the public towards Tony. I had a solicitor called Tim Jones who was going to work with me on the transaction, and I can't praise him enough for the role he played. I was the vehicle for the deal but he was the vital cog in the machine. Many people pay me a compliment regarding the survival of the club, but Tim worked harder than any other individual to save the Swans. There were other unsung heroes from this time too, such as Roger Wood, the manager of Natwest, without whose support I wouldn't have been able to commit myself financially as I did. A big thank you to him and my family solicitors T R Harris & Co, who recommended Tim to me initially. For the couple of months when the situation at Swansea City was critical I might as well have set a bed up in Tim's offices because I was there from early morning to very late at night.

Tim had given me his private number so that I could get hold of him at any time, because he understood the urgency of the situation. I rang at about six in the evening and he broke off from a presentation he was at in Clydach and met me at Briton Ferry roundabout, on the other side of the bridge. I jumped in his Jeep and we drove up to Cardiff with no time to spare. I didn't have the money with me, another group were travelling up with that and we did the deal together. I had agreed the figure with Tony Petty and I was brokering the deal, if you like. Tim and I got to the Copthorne Hotel late. We missed the turning because we were talking so much and were carrying on to Newport!

When we got there we thought the deal would have been done, but it hadn't as Tony wanted me present. The money was in a box on the table, under lock and key. There was a little bit of a stand-off and everyone was very serious. Once the deal was sealed I had a laugh to myself because I knew we were back in control. Tony Petty was gone, Mike Lewis was gone, and Don Goss took over the running of the club. We wanted to form a new board of directors, with new faces and the Supporters' Trust involved, and plant seeds for the future of Swansea City Football Club.

Where would the club be now if things had turned out differently? I believe we'd have gone out of the League. Look at Wrexham, Luton Town or Oxford – they're not coming back. Newport County? Do you honestly believe we'll ever see them back in the Football League? Wrexham were a lovely club, as were Newport, but they've gone downhill because everything collapses once you go out of the league.

The future ...

Swansea City today is doing a hell of a lot for Swansea *as* a city. The publicity is great – everyone in Spain knows who we are because of Roberto Martinez and the Spanish players. We are all very grateful for the job Roberto did for the club, and I am hopeful that Paulo Sousa will continue the good work. He has talked of turning Swansea City into a global brand and that is extremely positive, so I wish him well.

I'm pleased that we have Huw Jenkins as chairman. I've sat in Huw's company many times and seen him perform; I know that he won't allow his heart to rule his head. I've seen it all in football – the ups and the downs – and I've seen directors, very intelligent people like barristers, get carried away with themselves. The pressure from the general public and the supporters is tremendous. I've seen it first hand.

There are seven shareholders now and I remain one of them, for which I'm grateful as I'm still part of the club. I don't wish to get involved with the running of the club – I've had my day. Twice is enough and I don't want to go down that road a third time. It's lovely to see the club on a high as we head for 2010 and our centenary is just two years away. What a hundred years it's been! The stadium is fantastic and, although we share it with the Ospreys, the surface is fantastically well-maintained. I love to sit in my hotel lounge and listen to them on the television talking about our club; it brings bloody tears to my eyes. Top-flight managers say we are a Premiership club playing in the Championship – it's fantastic.

Also available from Y Lolfa:

£9.95

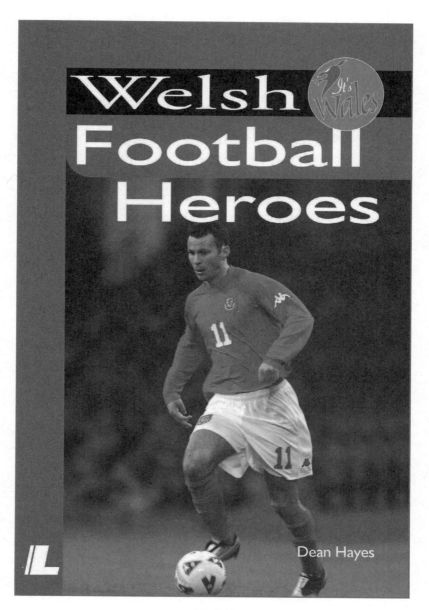

Welsh Football Heroes

Dean Hayes

£3.95

Mr Swansea: The Mel Nurse Story is just one of a whole range of publications from Y Lolfa. For a full list of books currently in print, send now for your free copy of our new full-colour catalogue.
Or simply surf into our website

www.ylolfa.com

for secure on-line ordering.

TALYBONT CEREDIGION CYMRU SY24 5HE
e-mail ylolfa@ylolfa.com
website www.ylolfa.com
phone (01970) 832 304
fax 832 782